CW00819736

FOUNTAINHEAD FOOD

cooking in andalucia

HELEN BARTLETT

FOUNTAINHEAD FOOD
cooking in andalucia

Copyright © Helen Bartlett 2012
Second Edition 2014

Published by Giant Mountain Publishing
www.giantmountainpublishing.com

ISBN 978-0-9566698-5-8

British Library Cataloguing in Publication Data
available on request

Printed and bound in Spain by Fullcolor Printcolor, Barcelona

GMP

FOUNTAINHEAD FOOD

cooking in andalucia

HELEN BARTLETT

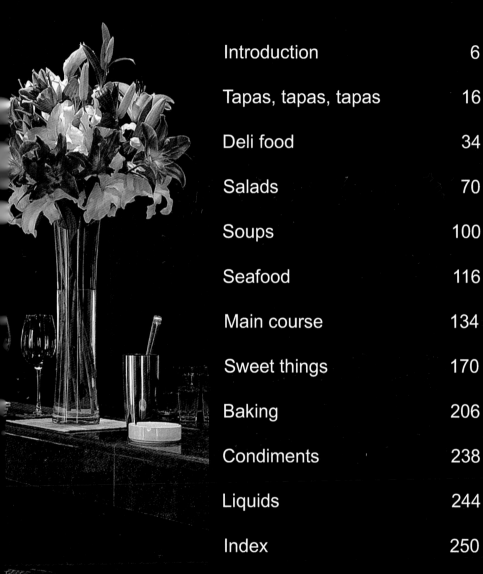

Contents

Introduction
Memories, Food and Andalucia

For as long as I can remember I have had a keen interest in food. This is without a doubt due to my mother who cooked with such care and thoughtfulness. She provided us with meals that always looked and tasted beautiful. However simple or plain - she always made an effort. She let us help her in the kitchen and spent time educating us on healthy eating and the importance of a balanced diet. As a little girl I would take her cookbooks to bed to read, although reading them was actually secondary – it was the pictures that interested me. I would look at them over and over, skimming the text and jotting down the main ingredients. At the weekends I would mess up the kitchen and do my own version (with varying degrees of success).

As my interest progressed I took more care to read the recipes. I quickly learned that some cooking (particularly baking at the time) needed exact proportions. I already really enjoyed chemistry so from then on experimenting with ingredients became part of my creative endeavours. Not being afraid was a very important key.

As the years went on I started to travel and to eat out. I have since been very privileged to have eaten in some truly amazing restaurants. I consequently moved on to chef's books, learning how to achieve more complex results, From learning the basics I would spend many a Saturday morning shopping in the local markets and gathering produce. Back in my kitchen I would happily cook for hours and hours preparing for a few dinner guests.

As I start writing, I question what this little book is going to be about? One of recipes and inspiring images or a 'restaurant chef' cook book? I decide on the former and divide my cooking into simple and complex – this is, after all, a land of contrasts, so I start with the straightforward. A visual book of less complicated recipes - those of colour, of life and of all nature has to offer, reflecting the simplicity of life here in Andalucia. The complex and more challenging restaurant dishes will be included in another collection.

One day in my life not so long ago, destiny called, literally drawing me purposefully to my spot. As an English woman in Andalucia I am, of course, an 'extranjero' - a foreigner, but I feel an affinity to the land and its people and from that very first day I have never felt anything but warmth in return. To the rest of Spain this may be peasant country but here the peasant is king – constantly aware of hard times, always adaptable and where his family, relations and friends are all more important than the outside world.

Within a short while of being here, I realized that I had planted myself in an enormous market garden. On the morning that I took my first walk here on our site, I brushed past wild fennel, its intense smell leaving me perfumed for hours. I walked in the almond groves, the trees laden with nuts. I found wild thyme, rosemary and lavender. I walked to sit at the top of the hill, passing carob and plum trees. Sitting gazing across the valley I could see white beehives dotted along its far contours. I sat then, on a stump that has since become a huge fig tree bearing some two hundred purple figs.

As the year went on the olives emerged, gathering weight on the trees – green ones, purple ones, black, oval, round, huge and small. The following spring I found hidden treasures, wild asparagus in thorny bushes and tiny crocuses guarding their jewels. I took a walk down the winding track to the river, past the pomegranate and eucalyptus trees. The valley lined with citrus groves - oranges, lemons and mandarins. Further along, market gardens full of avocado and mango trees. Everyman's plot standing proud with tomato vines, bamboo wigwams brimming with beans, cascading grapes and always that broken down old seat just to sit and enjoy his world. Walking back up the road from the village I passed the sweeping pink peppercorn trees and picked some to bring home. Along the track I found a caper plant and nearing our entrance three plants that sneak their fruit into view – the wild quince, fig and blackberry – if you blink you miss them.

Welcoming gifts arrived - bags of oranges, lemons, home brewed Malaga wine from the Muscatel and on our doorstep at Christmas, an enormous branch cut from a bay tree. A van honked its horn from the top of the far hill, drove down and sold us watermelons, onions and potatoes.

Almonds
I was to meet the corredor (a land negotiator) in a bar at 8.00am somewhere on the edge of town. No idea who I was looking for but his name was Domingo (Sunday in Spanish). I entered, the room fell silent – it was heaving men, full of smoke, cigarette papers littering the floor and a mass of glasses lining the bar. There was a strong aniseed smell and loud coughing. I tentatively walked up to the bar. A friendly looking man stood up from a table nearby and outstretched his hand. Domingo? He talked fast and gestured to go outside – I spoke no Spanish, he spoke no English. He waved and shouted goodbye to his friends. He beckoned me to follow and got in his van. I followed him in my hire car into the hills. We walked and climbed across hillsides, eventually sitting down under a tree as we waited for the owner to show up. He pottered about selecting some rocks, smoothing them, checking them over. He proceeded to pick almonds from the tree and showed me exactly how to crack them open, which ones were good and which were bad. They tasted creamy, yet were dry, intensely flavourful but subtle. They were my first real taste of Spain.

Fresh figs and coffee
The stump of a tree on which I sat a year before miraculously came back to life and bore its first new crop of figs. There was no water or electricity on site so I went to the village with an old jam jar and asked for it to be filled with hot espresso. Back at the top of the hill I sat drinking coffee from the jam jar and ate fresh figs. Something I still do today – coffee tastes better from glass and infinitely better with figs.

Fish
We sit outdoors overlooking the sea in a simple but pretty looking restaurant. We are approached by a large grubby looking chef. You like fish? There's no welcome, no hello. Yes we reply. He comes back alone (there are no staff). He puts a carafe of wine on the table, returns with a large bowl of salad and bread, He says nothing. Ten minutes later he comes back with two whole fish and some boiled potatoes. They were the best fish we had ever tasted.

Seafood
It was August and ninety-eight degrees. We had just arrived in a remote seaside town after a long journey. Unknown to us the local fiesta begins that evening. We had no accommodation booked and it was getting late. We ask around, the nice looking hotel is full – everywhere is full except one place has a back room, it's small, no bathroom, no window and no air-conditioning – we take it, leave our

bags and go in search of food. Everywhere by this time is alive with people. The restaurants are all full, it is dark and music starts to play in the distance. We pass a place that's packed but see a table free in the window – we go in and sit down quickly. The people are friendly and there's lots of shouting going on. A waiter approaches us – we have no idea what we are doing. He points to the board on the wall, presumably the menu - we point at one blindly. He disappears and within an instant returns with bread and wine. We are happy. Two minutes later he's back with our food, two enormous whole squid. Eyebrows raised, we have a go. Black ink spurts everywhere and the uncooked innards are all over our plates. Bon appetite! he says with a smile.

Eggs

Memories are not made by everything being perfect. It was a cold January night. We stopped at a very uninviting road side hostel. A large, bare white, fluorescent lit room – at one end, a small bar and in one corner, high on the wall a TV, the owner and his family huddled round. At the other end of the room a small dining area for guests. We had omelette and a glass of white wine – it was the most perfect meal.

Staff lunch

We gathered dried fennel sticks, almond twigs and stones. We set up under the large olive tree outside the kitchen in what we hope will one day become our 'huerta' – a kitchen garden worthy of the name. We make a trivet from three big stones and on it goes the pan with olive oil. I slice open thin green peppers, stuff them with fresh cheese and put them in the pan. They sizzle, blister and smoke. A few moments later we are sat on the ground eating them with sweet lemons and rosemary.

Olives

It is an unbelievable struggle. Our hills are for goats and we only have two legs – not only that, our feet are too large for the stony ground. I slide down a steep bank ripping my jeans, I laugh maniacally. I climb the tree and balance perilously on its branches holding a long stick. As I weld the stick high above my head I come dangerously close to falling. I don't know whether to laugh or cry – so I do both at once. The olives come down onto the net below, we forage in the grasses to pick every one up and load them into sacks. Forty five sacks later we take them to the mill. We follow their progress, watching eagerly as they transform themselves into a vibrant green, velvety liquid that is our unfiltered, cold pressed extra virgin olive oil - we use it in everything.

Fountainhead took four years to open its doors, emerging slowly from its wild hillside home. The buildings now start to merge into their backdrop as nature steps forth. The land is now naturally organic and starts to take a hold of us as we begin to live in a more harmonious way with it.

Cooking Notes

The recipes are on the whole for four people and assume a reasonable level of competence and familiarity with the process of cooking.

At first you may have to get used to my 'busy' approach to recipe writing. As with all recipes, it is a good idea to read through before beginning. Chefs in all restaurants work under pressure and usually there are many hands to do many different tasks. With one pair of hands in the home kitchen you need to adapt, working fast to achieve results. I don't cut corners but I take the most direct route. With your first recipe try something simple and short - as you get used to the way of working, you will hopefully find that you too can enjoy cooking without getting stuck in the kitchen!

The tapas section has no quantities and only outlines the recipes with all ingredients highlighted in green. Tapas is about improvisation - look at the pictures and be inspired to experiment. Some are traditional, the sort that can be found in bars across Andalucia. Others are simple combinations - often random choices of ingredients producing the most surprising results.

The deli section is like a shopfront full of ready made food and should be interpreted as such. The recipes produce a dish - feeding two if it's all you are eating, four when accompanied or six as a snack - in other words be flexible.

When reading the recipes assume to use as much homegrown, local and organic produce as possible. In the restaurant we use herbs in bunches that can be ten times bigger than those found in your average supermarket. They are always an integral part of the recipe so assume to use in generous quantities. The extra virgin olive oil is an essential ingredient for most dishes. Butter is used when necessary for its taste, enriching properties and consistency.

Cooking never takes up all of my time – most people have to spend a fair amount of time doing it – I just decided to really enjoy it!
Fountainhead January 2012

tapas, tapas, tapas

blanched vegetable skewer

smoked salmon, avocado on crostini

cauliflower, blackened peppers

assorted fruit skewer

mushroom, fried onions, toast

polenta, spinach, mozarella, pepper

19

Assorted vegetable skewer (p.18)

Trim the leeks, remove the outer layers and cut into short lengths (approx 2cm). Cook in boiling water for 2-3 minutes. Plunge immediately into cold water to retain colour and to prevent further cooking. Drain and set aside. Do the same for the mange tout, cooking for 30 seconds only. Shape the red pepper into small pieces and sauté gently in olive oil until tender. Briefly sauté the cherry tomatoes. Skewer the vegetables, drizzle with olive oil and season.

Smoked salmon, avocado, blackberry on crostini (p.18)

Cut small disks of bread and fry both sides in hot olive oil until golden. Season with salt and leave to cool on kitchen paper. Peel the avocado and shape the flesh into pieces. Squeeze with lemon juice to prevent colouring. Cut the smoked salmon into strips and roll up. Season well with freshly ground pepper. Construct the tapas using the crostini as a base. Add avocado, salmon and finish with blackberry. Drizzle with olive oil and sprinkle with sesame seeds.

Cauliflower, cheese béchamel, blackened peppers (p.18)

Trim the cauliflower into small florets and simmer in boiling water for about 7 minutes. Drain and set aside. Make a light béchamel sauce using single cream, infused bay leaf and grated cheese. Pour over the florets. Shape the red pepper into small pieces and sauté gently in olive oil until tender. Construct the tapas placing a piece of pepper on top of each floret, Secure with sticks, season with freshly ground black pepper.

Assorted fruit skewer (p.19)

Prepare fruits such as redcurrants, blackberries, watermelon, mango and pear. Cut the larger fruits into small cubes. Skewer, drizzle with lemon juice.

Mushrooms, oregano, fried onions, crostini (p.19)

Cut small disks of bread and fry both sides in hot olive oil until golden. Season with salt and leave to cool on kitchen paper. Clean the mushrooms, remove stalks and sauté both sides gently until golden brown. Season with oregano. Finely slice the onions and sauté on low heat until tender. Fill the mushrooms with heaped onions and secure on crostini with sticks.

Spinach, mozzarella, red pepper on polenta (p.19)

Cook a small amount of polenta and leave to set in a shallow container. Wilt the spinach in a pan with a little olive oil, season with salt and pepper. Shape the red pepper into small pieces and sauté over low heat until tender. Drain and thickly slice the mozzarella. Season the polenta and cut into small squares. Construct the tapas using the polenta as a base. Layer the spinach, mozzarella and pepper. Secure with sticks.

Little gem lettuces, pomegranate seeds, mild white onion (p.22)

Trim the lettuce, remove the outer leaves if necessary and cut in quarters lengthways. Peel and finely slice the white onion, scatter over the lettuce. Deseed the pomegranate and scatter over the lettuce. Finely chop a little garlic and sauté until golden in olive oil, scatter over the lettuce. Drizzle generously with olive oil

Dry marinated spiced chicken (p.22)

Cut the chicken breasts into long thick strips. In a large bowl put a tablespoon of flour, a tablespoon sweet pimiento, half a tablespoon of ground cumin, half a teaspoon each of salt, black pepper and ground cloves. Mix well. Place the chicken pieces into the dry marinade and coat each one thoroughly. Leave in for at least 3 hours. Juice one lemon and one orange. Sauté the chicken pieces in olive oil over medium heat for two minutes each side, reduce heat to the lowest setting, add the juices and fresh coriander leaves, cover with a lid or foil. Leave to cook gently for about 8 minutes turning once. Leave to stand for a further 2 minutes then slice thickly, drizzle with olive oil, garnish with pine nuts and serve warm.

Roasted peppers, garlic crostini (p.22)

Cut rounds from medium-thick slices of white bread. Make a small cut in each round of bread. Finely grate the garlic and insert a liitle into each piece of bread. Sauté in olive oil over medium heat until golden each side. Remove and place on kitchen paper to dry, season with salt. Cut small oval shapes from the flesh of the peppers and sauté in olive oil for a minute. Add a tablespoon of water and immediately cover. Turn down the heat and cook for about two minutes until just tender. Add some chopped basil. Skewer the pepper pieces onto the crostini.

little gem lettuce, pomegranate seeds, mild white onion

dry marinated chicken, pine nuts

roasted peppers, garlic crostini

asparagus, serrano ham, leek

marinated anchovies, herbs, olive oil

caviar, mascarpone, avocado

tomato, olive oil, toasted garlic crostini

black pudding. membrillo, crostini

< chorizo, scallions, crostini

25

Asparagus, Serrano ham, leeks (p.23)

Trim the asparagus ends. Steam the tips for approximately 3 minutes then immediately plunge into cold water and drain. Trim the leeks, remove the outer layers, cut into long strips and blanch in boiling water for 3 minutes. Wrap small bundles of asparagus tips in thin slices of serrano ham and an outer layer of leek. Secure with sticks. Drizzle with olive oil, season with salt and pepper.

Anchovies, olive oil, herbs (p.23)

The anchovies used in this tapas are marinated (usually in oil) as opposed to the salted type and are readily available in Spain. Simply drain the anchovies from their marinade, dab dry. Finely chop parsley and a little mild onion. Sprinkle over the anchovies, season with freshly ground black pepper, squeeze a little lemon juice and drizzle generously with olive oil.

Caviar, avocado, mascarpone (p.23)

Cut rounds from medium-thick slices of white bread. Sauté in olive oil over medium heat until golden each side. Remove and place on kitchen paper to dry, season with salt. Peel the avocado and cut into thick slices, season with black pepper. Place a spoonful of mascarpone on top and garnish with caviar. Drizzle with olive oil and lemon juice.

Tomatoes, garlic, olive oil bread (p.24)

Finely chop the tomatoes, add a small quantity of finely chopped mild onion, season with salt and pepper. Put in a container with all the juices, drizzle generously with olive oil and leave to stand. Finely slice the garlic cloves and shallow fry in olive oil until golden. Use a pastry cutter to cut thick rounds of rustic type bread. Fry in olive oil until golden on both sides. Drain the tomatoes and spoon onto the fried bread. Sprinkle with fried garlic.

Chorizo, scallions, crostini (p.24-25)

Cut rounds from medium-thick slices of white bread. Sauté in olive oil over medium heat until golden each side. Remove and place on kitchen paper to dry, season with salt. Cut the chorizo (fresh variety) into thick slices and sauté both sides gently in olive oil. Place a piece on each crostini. Slice the scallions and position on top.

Black pudding, membrillo, crostini (p.25)

Cut rounds from medium-thick slices of white bread. Saute in olive oil over medium heat until golden each side. Remove and place on kitchen paper to dry, season with salt. Cut the black pudding into thick slices and sauté both sides gently in olive oil. Place a piece on each crostini and add a spoonful of membrillo on top, sprinkle with finely chopped rosemary. Membrillo is a heavy set quince paste / jam that we make from the wild quince in the autumn (p.240). Other types of jams or jellies work well such as apple or greengage. Serve warm.

Herb tartlets (p.28)

Prepare some simple pastry using plain flour, olive oil a pinch of salt and a splash of warm water. Bring it together to a good dough consistency. Divide into small balls and press each one into small oiled tart tins (any shape, individual or a tray) making sure the pastry is not too thick. Trim the edges if necessary. Bake in a hot oven for 5 minutes or until just coloured. Cut the cheese (fresh cheese is best) into medium thick slices and trim to fit into the tarts. Slice the tomatoes and grill for 30 seconds each side (or sauté in olive oil for 10 seconds each side). Place a slice of tomato in each tart, season with salt and pepper. Cover each with a slice of cheese and put under the grill for approx 1 minute. Sprinkle generously with herbs such as rosemary and thyme, including their flowers if you have them. Serve warm.

Morcilla, apple, sage, beans (p.29)

Prepare or cook the beans - (any will do, for example haricot or pinto). Peel the apple, cut into small cubes and gently sauté in olive oil until soft, stir in fresh sage leaves and season. Cut the morcilla (black pudding) into thick slices and gently sauté on both sides in olive oil. Toss all together and serve warm.

Aubergines with cane syrup (p.29)

Make a light batter using eggs, flour and milk. Cut the aubergine into slices (approx 0.5cm thick). Dip the aubergine slices in the batter and shallow fry on medium to high heat in olive oil, turn if necessary, remove and season sparingly with salt. Drizzle with cane syrup, (molasses or maple syrup as an alternative), serve immediately.

< herb, tomato tartlets

black pudding, beans, apple, sage

aubergines, cane syrup, pine nuts

< artichokes, tomato, herbs   scallop, rosemary, pimiento

spanish omelette

Artichoke hearts, shallots, tomatoes, garlic (p.30)

Remove the outer layers of the artichokes, cook in boiling water for approximately 7 minutes. Drain. Finely chop the shallots and sauté gently in olive oil until tender. Finely chop the tomatoes and add to the shallots. Continue to sauté for about 1 minute. Add finely chopped fresh thyme. Cut the artichokes lengthways, pile a spoonful of tomato mixture on top of each half. Season with salt and pepper and drizzle with olive oil.

Scallops, pimiento, rosemary (p.31)

Open the fresh scallop shells, carefully remove the scallops and clean, making sure to remove the waste strip. Sear in olive oil over medium heat for 2 – 3 minutes turning over constantly. Drizzle more olive oil as they cook, add ground pimiento, and chopped fresh rosemary. Serve immediately.

Spanish omelette (p.31)

Proportions 6 eggs, 2 medium sized potatoes, I green pepper. Peel the potatoes, dice and cook in boiling water until tender. Drain and set aside. Finely slice the green pepper and sauté gently in olive oil for a few minutes. Whisk the eggs together, add the cooked potatoes and cooked peppers. Season well. This omelette needs to be cooked thick so for the quantities above you will only need a medium sized frying pan. Pre heat the olive oil in the frying pan and add the egg mixture. Turn down the heat to low and slowly cook the omelette for approx 5 minutes. To cook the top side, place under the grill (not too close) for another 5 minutes. Leave to stand. Serve warm or cold.

Tuna, courgette, mango (p.33)

Cut the fresh tuna into small cubes. Slice rounds of courgette (approx 1cm thick). Peel the mango and shape the flesh into small rounded pieces. Sauté the courgettes in olive oil on medium heat until soft and coloured on each side, season with freshly ground black pepper and set aside. Rapidly sear the tuna cubes in olive oil on high heat, turn quickly. Turn out and drizzle generously with olive oil and lemon juice. Construct the tapas using the courgette as a base, complete with tuna, mango and sprigs of dill.

Contents

deli food

Sun dried tomato and fresh cheese tart

In this recipe the tomatoes and cheese are grilled just before serving and placed on top of the pastry base. In the restaurant during the summer we sun dry our tomatoes outside and use on the day. The resulting tomatoes have a greatly enhanced flavour, both intense and sweet but still tasting fresh. If you don't have hot enough weather to do this you could put the tomatoes in the oven.

6 medium vine tomatoes
1 bunch basil leaves
400g fresh artisan cheese

Baby salad leaves
(spinach, lambs lettuce or rocket)

For the pastry
Chives
400g plain flour
Pine nuts (toasted)
200ml extra virgin olive oil
Extra virgin olive oil
1 teaspoon sugar
Salt
1 teaspoon salt
Freshly ground black pepper
70ml water

To sun dry the tomatoes, allow 6 hours advance preparation. Cut the tops off the tomatoes and slice. Place on an oven tray, drizzle with olive oil and season with a little salt. Leave in direct sun for about 3 hours then turn them over, leaving again for about 3 hours. The tomatoes will shrink. When ready the tomatoes should be moist, not dried to a crisp. Transfer the tomatoes to a dish. If you can't do this put them in the oven on 100° for a couple of hours each side.

Pre heat the oven to 220°C. To make the pastry, put the flour into a large bowl, mix in the salt and sugar. Add the olive oil and water, bring together with the hands until it 'holds'. Do not over work. Form small balls, flatten and press into individual oiled tart tins. Work with the fingers to mould a fine layer of pastry. Bake in the oven until golden (5 - 7 minutes). Remove and leave to cool in the tins.

To construct the tarts, position a pastry case in the centre of each serving plate. Finely slice the basil. Slice the cheese, season and drizzle with olive oil. Place the dried tomatoes (in small portion-sized piles) on a baking tray. Distribute the sliced basil onto the piles of tomatoes. Layer the cheese slices on top and place under a hot grill for 2 minutes. Transfer each pile to a tart base. Place the baby leaves on top, scatter the pine nuts and chives, drizzle with olive oil and serve.

Photo note. For colour, add a little parsley oil (p.240) and fresh tomato juices to the plates before arranging.

Partridge terrine

2 chicken breasts (uncooked)
4 partridges (uncooked)
16 rashers bacon (finely sliced)
3 fresh bay leaves
1 tablespoon fresh thyme leaves
2 juniper berries (crushed)
250ml double cream

2 shallots
1 clove garlic
20 pink peppercorns
2g gelatine (sheets or powder)
Sea salt
Freshly ground pepper

Pre heat the oven to 220°C. Soak the peppercorns in a little hot water for 15 minutes. For this recipe you will need an oven proof terrine dish. Line this with cling film, leaving a generous overlap on all edges. Lay in the strips of bacon across the base and up the sides, overlap slightly and line the ends.

Dice the chicken, put in a food processor and season well. Finely chop the shallots and garlic, add to the chicken. Add the thyme, juniper and cream. Blend until smooth. Prepare the partridges. Remove the breasts and any leg meat, discard the skin. Slice the breasts horizontally in half. Spoon some prepared chicken meat into the terrine, spread an even layer over the bottom. Drop in some peppercorns. Place half of the partridge meat on top to form the next layer. Repeat another layer of each meat until all the meat is used. Place some more bacon and two bay leaves on the top of the terrine. Draw up the cling film from over the sides and overlap to seal. Cover with tin foil.

The terrine needs to be cooked gently in a Bain Marie to prevent burning. Simply place the terrine dish in a deeper, larger dish or oven tray. Fill this with cold water (should come ¾ way up sides of terrine dish). Cover the whole thing with more foil and place in the middle of a hot oven for 1 hour. When done the terrine should be firm. Leave to cool a little. Remove the terrine dish and snip the cling film at both ends, Drain the juices into a bowl. Press the terrine (weigh down - full juice or milk cartons do this well) then refrigerate overnight. In a small pan, heat the juices over a low heat, add the last bay leaf and gelatine, stir until dissolved. Pour into a container to set.

To serve. Turn the terrine upside down and remove the wrappings. With a very sharp knife cut into slices. Serve with the bay jelly and plum and fig chutney p.242.

Char grilled vegetable salad with wild thyme dressing

4 baby green peppers (whole)
2 leeks
1 yellow pepper
1 red pepper
2 courgettes
6 runner beans
8 small button mushrooms
12 cherry tomatoes

For the dressing
1 teaspoon coarse grain mustard
20ml white wine vinegar
50ml extra virgin olive oil
1 clove garlic
1 lemon
2 dessertspoons caster sugar
1 tablespoon wild thyme leaves
Pinch of salt
Freshly ground black pepper

To prepare the dressing, finely zest and juice the lemon. Put the juice, vinegar, thyme leaves and sugar into a pan. Place on low heat to infuse. Heat until the sugar has dissolved. Finely grate the garlic and add to the pan, remove from the heat. Whisk in the mustard, lemon zest, and olive oil. Season with salt and pepper.

Trim the leeks and beans and cut diagonally into 4cm lengths. De-seed the peppers and shape each into 8 pieces. Slice the courgettes diagonally (approximated 0.5cm thick). Trim the mushrooms. Put a large pan of water on to boil. Simmer the leeks for 3 minutes, plunge immediately into cold water, drain and set aside. Do the same for the beans, cooking for 30 seconds only.

Pre heat the char grill for 7 minutes. Char grill the vegetables in batches, turning after a minute or until they have blackened marks. Char grilling the peppers will just soften them. If you prefer them better cooked, put them to sweat in a sealed container or a plastic bag directly after grilling. Arrange all the vegetables in a dish, drizzle with the dressing and serve warm or cold.

Seared swordfish with green peppers, red currants and chives

We buy our swordfish in large chunks which are a quarter section of whole big fish - it is fantastically fresh. Most Spanish restaurants serve this fish thinly sliced on the bone with lemon and oil. It is a perfect way of serving such fresh fish. In our version here, we cut the fish as if it were meat and sear it in extra virgin olive oil. The resulting succulent fish is complemented by the tartness of the redcurrants, the subtlty of the chives and the flavourful peppers.

250g swordfish (no skin, no bones)
2 green peppers
30 red currants
1 bunch chives
1 lemon
2 tablespoons extra virgin olive oil
Coarse sea salt
Freshly ground black pepper

Cut the swordfish into thin slices and season with pepper. Remove the redcurrants from their stalks. Juice the lemon. Cut the chives into 5cm lengths. De-seed the peppers and cut into oval shapes. Heat 1 tablespoon olive oil in a shallow pan, sauté the peppers on high for about 2 minutes. Remove from the pan, put in a sealed container or plastic bag to sweat. Add the swordfish to the pan with a little more olive oil and sear for 1 minute on each side until golden, add the lemon juice. Turn out into a serving dish with all the juices, add the green peppers, red currants and chives. Drizzle with olive oil and season with sea salt. Serve immediately,

Bombay potatoes with lime, garlic and tomatoes

This dish makes a tasty, economical meal on its own. The addition of the 'al dente' garlic and peppers to the soft potato and tomato mix are as important as the combination and addition of lime and salt. Alternative spices and chillies could be added.

6 medium sized potatoes
2 green peppers
2 red onions
4 medium vine tomatoes
3 limes
8 cloves garlic
2 teaspoons ground coriander spice
1 teaspoon ground cardamom
Coarse sea salt
Freshly ground black pepper
Fresh coriander leaves
Extra virgin olive oil

Peel the potatoes and cut into cubes, around 1cm. Bring a large pan of water to the boil and drop in the potatoes. Boil for 2 minutes or until just done. Strain and immediately plunge into cold water to prevent further cooking. Strain again and leave to dry. Finely slice the onion. De-seed the peppers and finely slice. Finely chop the garlic. Zest the limes in fine strips and juice. Finely dice the tomatoes (retain the juices). In a large heavy bottomed pan, heat the oil. Add the onions and sauté for 3 minutes but do not brown. Stir in the cooked potatoes. Turn up the heat and rapidly stir in the tomatoes (with juice), peppers, garlic and lime zest. Stir and cook for a few minutes until the tomatoes soften and the potatoes start to lose their shape. Add the spices and lime juice, season well and turn out into a serving dish, garnish generously with coriander leaves.

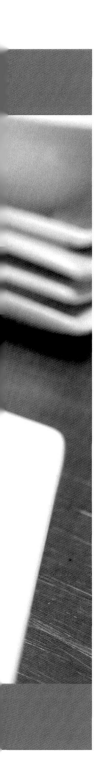

Seared squid, scallions, chilli and coriander

Squid has a unique flavour and texture that are the essence of this dish. Searing the squid on high heat helps to keep it tender and gives it colour and bite. It is also important to let it stand as this helps to keep it soft. Its particular flavour is enhanced by the pungency of chillies, the fragrance of coriander and the strong leafy taste of scallions.

4 small squid cleaned
2 cloves garlic
2 scallions (spring onions)
4 chillies
1 bunch fresh coriander
2 limes
1 large sweet orange
1 tablespoon caster sugar
4 tablespoons extra virgin olive oil
1 tablespoon white wine vinegar
Freshly ground black pepper
Salt

To make the dressing, finely zest and juice the orange. Put the juice and sugar into a small pan, put on low heat and cook for 1 minute. Stir in the vinegar, orange zest and 2 tablespoons olive oil. Chop the coriander stalks, add to the pan. Zest and juice the limes.

De-seed and finely slice the chillies. Slice the scallions. Finely chop the garlic. Cut the squid lengthways and into thick slices. Dry the pieces thoroughly and season. Heat 2 tablespoons olive oil in a shallow pan until very hot. Add the squid pieces carefully. Stir fry over high heat for about 3 minutes until they start to colour. Turn the heat down, quickly stir in the chillies, garlic, scallions, lime zest, lime juice and most of the coriander leaves. Cover immediately, remove from heat and leave to stand for at least 3 minutes. Turn the squid out into a serving dish. Pour over the dressing, garnish with the rest of the coriander leaves and serve immediately.

Shredded vegetable filo parcels

These make a tasty snack at any time of day. Other groups of complementary vegetables, herbs and spices work just as well. For example, you could combine aubergine, onion, tomato and cumin or spinach, mushroom, garlic and parsley.

12 sheets filo pastry
1 leek
1 courgette
2 carrots
4 runner beans
1 lemon
6 stems fresh coriander
2 tablespoons extra virgin olive oil
Freshly ground pepper
Salt
1 egg, mixed to glaze

Remove the outer layer from the leek. Peel the carrots. Trim the courgettes and beans. Slice all the vegetables lengthways and cut into thin sticks about 5cm long. In a large pan heat the oil, stir fry the vegetables on medium heat for about 2 minutes. Add the lemon juice and turn out to cool. Finely chop the coriander and stir into the vegetables, season. Lay out a sheet of filo, place a spoonful of vegetables in the centre, brush on a little egg around the edges, fold in and layer to seal the parcel, glaze the top. Repeat.

These parcels can be cooked in a hot oven for about 5 minutes or shallow   fried in olive oil until golden. Serve with raita p.243.

Seared tuna, scallions, wilted chicory, ginger and orange

This is another fish that we buy in a large lump that is wonderfully fresh - straight off the boat. It is an extremely meaty fish and is best served rare. We sear the whole pieces just as you would do a beef fillet, and like meat it benefits from being well seasoned. Tuna has an affinity with orange and ginger - the chicory has a slippery texture and a faint bitterness that balance the dish well.

500g piece tuna loin (skinless, boneless)
3 heads yellow chicory
2 scallions (spring onions)
Fresh ginger root (6cm length)
1 clove garlic
1 lime
1 large orange
1 dessertspoon caster sugar
Extra virgin olive oil
Coarse sea salt
Freshly ground black pepper

Prepare the tuna. The aim here is to cut and shape your lump of tuna into pieces that are about 7cm long and are cylindrical in shape - with a diameter of about 5cm. It doesn't matter if they are not perfectly shaped - it's just an approximate size for cooking. Season your pieces generously with salt and pepper.

To make the dressing, finely zest and juice the orange and lime. Put the juices in a small pan with the sugar and heat gently until dissolved. Peel and grate the ginger and the garlic, add to the pan. Remove from the heat, add the zests, stir and leave to infuse.

Finely slice the scallions diagonally. Prepare the chicory. Cut off the hard end and separate the leaves. Place in a large shallow pan and sauté on high heat in two tablespoons olive oil. Turn the leaves over, cooking until wilted and just starting to colour. Turn out into a serving dish, season with pepper. Put the pan back on the heat, add the tuna pieces, searing on all sides. Turn and cook for about one minute. Remove from the pan and leave to sit for one more minute.

To serve, thickly slice the tuna pieces and layer over the chicory, pour over the dressing, scatter the scallions and serve.

Roasted poussin stuffed with prunes, thyme and apricots

This is a great supper or light lunch dish. It is easy to prepare in advance and good hot or cold. If using chickens instead of poussins, double the quantities. Serve with crusty bread and a simple green leaf salad.

2 whole poussin
1 red onion
2 cloves garlic
½ small aubergine
50g organic dried apricots
50g organic prunes (stoneless)
2 slices white bread
2 teaspoons dried thyme leaves
1 teaspoon fresh rosemary
Extra virgin olive oil
Sea salt
Freshly ground black pepper
Mild green chilli or pepper

Pre heat the oven to 220°C. Finely chop the onion and garlic. Sauté on low heat in a little olive oil until tender, set aside. Dice the aubergine (remove the skin if tough and discard). Sauté on high heat until golden. Finely slice the apricots and prunes. Finely chop the rosemary. Cut the bread up into small pieces and put into a food processor. Blend to crumbs. Add the onion, aubergine, prunes, apricots, garlic, thyme and rosemary. Pulse to a rough paste. Season well and pulse again. Stuff the poussin cavities with the paste. Line an oven tray with foil with a double layer and a generous overhang on all sides. Drizzle generously with olive oil. Place the birds on top, drizzle again with oil, season well and wrap the birds up in the foil but do not completely seal. Bake for 40 minutes.

Remove and leave to cool. Take a very sharp knife and cut right down the centre of each bird. Arrange in a dish, garnish with fine strips of mild green chilli. or pepper.

Spring vegetables with bay infused vinaigrette

Here we have ordinary vegetables, each one sweet, tender, powerful and full of flavour - we are lucky because these are our local produce. For this dish with produce like this you hardly need to do a thing. They deserve to be served on their own with a glass of chilled white.

2 leeks	2 fresh bay leaves
2 turnips	100ml extra virgin olive oil
2 carrots	15ml white wine vinegar
1 yellow pepper	1 lemon
1 courgette	2 teaspoons grain mustard
4 small green peppers	2 teaspoons orange blossom honey
12 mange tout	Coarse sea salt
12 green beans	Freshly ground black pepper

For the vinaigrette, juice the lemon and put into a pan with the vinegar, honey and bay leaves. Heat gently to infuse for 5 minutes. Stir in the grain mustard and one tablespoon olive oil. Season generously.

Pccl the carrots and turnips, trim the leeks and mange tout, and shape all into neat pieces. Leave the baby peppers whole. Trim the beans and cut into short lengths. Bring a large saucepan of water to the boil, add one tablespoon olive oil to the water and blanch the prepared turnip pieces for about 1 minute 30 seconds – remove and plunge immediately into cold water, drain and set aside. In the same way, blanch the carrot and leek pieces for 1 minute and the mange tout and beans for 30 seconds. Put the green peppers, with one tablespoon olive oil into a shallow pan on low heat. Sauté gently for 3 minutes without browning. Turn into a dish, cover and leave to sweat. Sauté the yellow peppers and courgette pieces for 2 minutes. Remove from heat.

To serve, gently mix all the vegetables together and drizzle with the bay infused vinaigrette.

Broad beans, parsley and Serrano ham

This is a classic Spanish dish which is simplicity itself. Using fresh beans makes a difference as does the quality of ham - make sure your piece has little or no fat. There is no need to season with salt as most hams have a salty edge that complements the beans perfectly.

250g fresh broad beans (out of their pods)
150g lump Serrano ham
1 bunch parsley
1 mild white Spanish onion
15ml white wine vinegar
30ml extra virgin olive oil
Freshly milled black pepper

Put a large pan of water on to boil. Cook the beans rapidly for about 5 minutes, drain and plunge into cold water, Remove the outer pale skins to reveal the green inner bean. Drain and put in a large bowl. Cut the ham into short, thin sticks. Finely chop the parsley and white onion and stir into the beans. Mix the vinegar and olive oil, season generously with black pepper and pour over the beans. Keeps for three days when refrigerated.

White and green beans with shallots

This is a lovely combination of ingredients that are very popular in Spain. You can pre cook the white beans or, if you search, you can find beans in jars with nothing added, making this dish very quick and simple to prepare.

200g white butter / haricot beans (cooked)
200g French beans
3 vine tomatoes
4 shallots
1 lemon
1 teaspoon smooth mustard
1 teaspoon orange blossom honey
100ml extra virgin olive oil
Freshly ground black pepper
Salt

Finely chop the shallots, sauté gently in a little olive oil (without browning) until just soft. Set aside to cool. Trim the green beans and cut into short lengths. Blanch in boiling water for 30 seconds. Plunge into cold water quickly to prevent further cooking, drain and dry. Finely dice the tomatoes, put in a large bowl, season with a little salt. Add the cooked white beans and season generously with black pepper. Juice the lemon and combine thoroughly with the mustard and honey. Add 2 tablespoons of olive oil and pour over the beans. Stir in the shallots and tip out into a serving dish.

Fishcakes

Always one of the most popular orders - we have been making these like this for quite a while - sometimes varying the recipe using different fish, herbs and spices but we always come back to this. If you like them extra zingy, double the ginger and lemon zest.

500g fish pieces(such as salmon, tuna, cod)
1 mild white onion
Fresh ginger root (4cm length)
Fresh coriander leaves (6 stalks)
1 tablespoon fresh smooth tomato ketchup p.243
1 small bunch fresh coriander
300g peeled waxy potatoes
1 lemon
50g white bread
50g polenta
2 eggs
Extra virgin olive oil

Finely chop the white onion and coriander leaves. Peel and finely grate the ginger root. Finely zest and juice the lemons. Put a pan of water on to boil. Cut the potato into similar sized pieces and boil until soft. Drain and mash thoroughly whilst hot. If necessary, remove the bones and skin from the fish, cut into fillets or small pieces. Heat a little olive oil in a shallow pan on low heat, add the fish pieces, cover and sauté very gently with minimal browning until cooked. Set aside to cool slightly. Remove the fish from the pan, put in a large bowl and flake with a fork or fingers. Add the mashed potato, tomato ketchup, raw white onion, grated ginger, lemon zest and juice. Bring together and mix thoroughly to form a stiff paste. Refrigerate for 20 minutes.

Put the bread (in small pieces) and polenta into the food processor and grind to fine crumbs. In a separate bowl whisk the eggs and 1 tablespoon olive oil together,

Remove the fish paste from the refrigerator and form into small balls (about 3cm in diameter). Dip each one carefully in the egg mixture and then roll in the breadcrumb and polenta mix, coat thoroughly. Repeat. These fishcakes can be refrigerated until ready to cook as they are best cooked fresh.

To serve, shallow fry the fishcakes in olive oil, carefully turning until golden all over. Serve with chilli and coriander salsa see p 241.

Boletus tartlets, tarragon and rosemary flowers

These wild mushrooms have a fabulous flavour not disimilar to almonds - they are easy to prepare and require very little cleaning. A small amount of butter enhances their luscious texture when cooked.

400g plain flour
200ml extra virgin olive oil
1 teaspoon sugar
1 teaspoon salt
70ml water

250g Boletus
1 tablespoon extra virgin olive oil
25g unsalted butter
1 bunch tarragon leaves
1 teaspoon rosemary flowers

Pre heat the oven to 220°C. To make the pastry, put the flour into a large bowl, mix in the salt and sugar. Add the olive oil and water, bring together with the hands until it 'holds'. Do not over work. Form small balls, flatten and press into individual oiled tart tins. Work with the fingers to mould a fine layer of pastry to the base and sides. Bake in the oven until golden (about 5 minutes). Remove, leave to cool in the tins.

Slice the boletus, sauté in olive oil and butter until soft and coloured, add the tarragon leaves and season well, Spoon into the tarts, scatter the rosemary flowers. Carefully remove the filled tarts from the tins. Serve immediately.

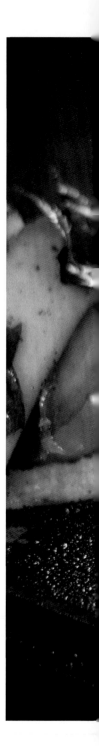

Lebanese meatballs, red onions, cumin and lime

This is a heart warming dish to serve at any time of the year, as a main meal with creamed potatoes or individually as a tapas. It has strong flavours and bold combinations - the lamb and the pungent cumin are cut by the piquant pimiento and the sharpness of lime.

250g lamb meat (with minimal fat)
2 medium onions
1 teaspoon ground cumin
1 dessert spoon pimiento
1 tablespoon plain flour
Half teaspoon thyme (fresh or dry)
2 teaspoons cumin seeds
3 limes
Large handful of fresh coriander leaves
4 tomatoes
1 large orange
1 egg
Extra virgin olive oil
Salt
Freshly ground black pepper

Cut the meat into small cubes. Finely chop the onions and the tomatoes (retain the juices). Zest and juice the limes and the orange. Put the meat, 1 tablespoon of the chopped onions, the ground cumin, 1 teaspoon cumin seeds and the egg into the food processor. Pulse and combine to form a mince - check as you pulse as too much will result in a paste. Remove and form into balls about 3cm in diameter.

Combine the flour and pimiento and roll each ball in the mix, covering thoroughly. In a deep frying pan sauté the meat balls in olive oil for a few minutes until lightly browned all over. Stir gently, turn the heat down and add all the rest of the ingredients. Season with salt and pepper, cover and simmer on low heat for a further 10 minutes. Stir carefully from time to time.

Serve with Greek yoghurt and harissa (p.240).

Marinated salmon, lemon, chives and dill

This ia a wonderful summery dish that can be prepared well in advance. It goes well with fragrant rice salad p.81 and green leaves.

4 salmon fillets (cut from one side, no skin, no bones)
½ white onion
2 lemons
1 teaspoon smooth mustard
Fresh root ginger (2cm length)
1 teaspoon sugar
1 small bunch fresh dill
1 small bunch chives
Extra virgin olive oil
Freshly ground black pepper

Finely zest and juice the lemons. Finely chop the white onion, dill and chives. Peel and finely grate the ginger. Put the lemon juice and sugar into a small pan, put on low heat until the sugar dissolves. Add the grated ginger and mustard, mix and leave to infuse. Heat 1 tablespoon olive oil in a shallow pan on high heat. Carefully add the salmon fillets and sear the bottoms, turn the heat to low, add 2 tablespoons water, cover immediately. Leave to steam for about 3 minutes, remove the pan from the heat and carefully place the salmon fillets into a serving dish. Pour over the ginger infusion, drizzle generously with olive oil, sprinkle with lemon zest, chopped onion and herbs, season with pepper. Seal the dish with cling film and leave to cool. Serve cold.

Note. Depending on your cut of salmon, particularly its thickness, you may find it easier (safer) to leave the skin on, as without it, once cooked it can easily break apart if not handled with care..

Pork with sage, garlic and sweet lemons

The pork in Spain is some of the best you will find anywhere and it is eaten all over Andalucia. Cooked simply with classic Mediterranean flavours it is best eaten with rustic bread and extra virgin olive oil - perfect!

250g pork fillet
1 red onion
1 sweet lemon
3 cloves garlic
20 sage leaves
120ml extra virgin olive oil
Salt
Freshly ground black pepper

Pre heat the oven to 200°C. Finely slice the red onions. Using a potato peeler remove the zest from the lemon and cut into fine strips. Juice the lemon. Season the pork loin generously with salt and pepper. Line a small oven tray with foil and add two tablespoon olive oil, place the sliced onions on top and then the meat. Place more foil over to cover but do not completely seal. Bake for 20 minutes, remove and leave to stand. Finely slice the garlic and sauté in 2 tablespoons olive oil until golden. Remove from the pan, add the sage leaves, sauté rapidly until crisp. Remove quickly and leave to dry on kitchen paper.

To serve, cut the pork into slices, pour over the meat juices, scatter with the onions, garlic, sage and lemon zest. Season well. Drizzle geneously with lemon juice and olive oil.
Note. Sweet lemons come in winter and have a thick pithy skin and sweeter juice. If you can´t find them, substitute normal ones. If you want to sweeten these, drop the zest strips into a pan with one tablespoon sugar and one tablespoon water, heat briefly to a light syrup and leave to stand. Add when serving the dish.

Contents

salads

Salad of white crab, pawpaw, avocado, scallions and lime

The textures of paw paw and avocado are similar, together they are a subtle and cleansing combination. The crab adds a taste of the sea and a contrast in texture. The ginger and lime are a perfect complement to all three.

200g fresh white crab meat
1 paw paw
1 avocado
1 large scallion
Chives
2 limes
Fresh ginger root (6cm length)
50g caster sugar
50ml water
Frisée lettuce
Freshly milled pepper
Extra virgin olive oil

The fruits for this dish must be in perfect condition and need to be prepared just before serving as they easily brown. Put the sugar into a small pan with the water and put on low heat. Peel the ginger root, finely grate and add to the pan. Simmer gently for 30 seconds. Set aside to cool. Prepare the frisée choosing only the most delicate leaves. Remove the outer layer from the scallion and finely slice. Finely zest and juice the limes. Carefully remove the skin from the fruits. Cut in half and remove the stone from the avocado and pips from the pawpaw. Cut the flesh into medium-thick slices and drizzle with a little lime juice. Put the crab meat in a bowl, season well with black pepper, stir in the lime zest.

To serve, arrange the avocado and paw paw slices alternately, overlapping each other. Season with black pepper and drizzle with olive oil. Layer the crab meat, frisée and scallions on top. Drizzle with the ginger syrup, lime juice and more olive oil. Scatter with chives. Serve immediately. Goes well with a chilled crisp slightly floral white wine such as a Verdejo from Rueda.

Char grilled sweet potato, red onion, tomato, lime and coriander

We make this dish when the tomatoes are very ripe and literally dropping off the vines. It takes a while to prepare but is well worth the effort.- its vibrant colours and flavours always remind us of the hot Andalucian summers.

2 medium sweet potatoes
1 red onion
4 ripe vine tomatoes
2 limes
1 bunch coriander
1 teaspoon orange blossom honey
50ml extra virgin olive oil
Coarse sea salt
Freshly ground black pepper

For this dish it is necessary to remove the tomato skins. If your tomatoes aren't sun-ripened, it is best to blanch them for a minute, then leave them to sit in the hot water for a further 5 minutes. The skins will become easy to remove. If you are lucky enough to be able to pick your own, choose the ripest - the skins will come off easily without having to cut into the flesh. Cut the flesh from the tomatoes working around the core, cut into oval shapes and season with pepper.

Put a large pan of water on to boil. Boil the sweet potatoes for 5 minutes, remove and put in a plastic bag, seal and leave to sweat for 5 minutes. Take the potato out of the bag, remove the skin and cut into medium thick slices. Heat the char gill for 7 minutes and grill the potato pieces, char each side, season with salt.

Use a potato peeler to peel the zest from the limes – finely slice the zest and juice the limes. Ultra-finely slice the onion. To make the dressing, take the tomato cores and put into a conical sieve, press out the juices. Retain, add the lime juice and honey, mix thoroughly.

To construct the salad, layer the char grilled potato slices with the tomato, pour over the dressing. Garnish generously with fresh coriander leaves, raw onion slices and lime zest, drizzle with olive oil and serve.

Strawberry, chilli and rocket salad

The strawberry season starts in early February as the almond blossom falls from the trees. It marks the point when spring is truly with us. Rocket is available all year round in many varieties. For this dish we use smaller, peppery leaves that are not over hot, Strawberries and rocket are a divine match - the chilli dressing and dill simply make them zing!

100g rocket
6 large ripe strawberries
2 large fresh red chillies (mild)
1 lime
1 medium vine tomato
1 heaped tablespoon sugar
50ml olive oil
Fresh ginger root (3cm length)
Fresh dill sprigs
Extra virgin olive oil

To make the dressing. Finely zest and juice the lime. Peel and finely grate the ginger root. De-seed the chillies and finely slice. Roughly chop the tomato and put in a small pan with the lime juice (include all the tomato juices). Add the sugar and put on low heat until the sugar has dissolved. Strain through a conical sieve, retaining the liquid. Add the lime zest, chillies and ginger to the liquid and leave to infuse for at least 10 minutes. Add olive oil. De-stalk the strawberries and slice. To serve, arrange the strawberries and rocket, pour over the chilli dressing, drizzle with olive oil and garnish generously with small sprigs of dill.

Serrano ham, fresh figs, quail eggs and summer leaves with red onion dressing

For this we use our young beetroot tops and Toscana negro from our kitchen garden but any summer leaves such as baby spinach, red oak, chicory or rocket would all go equally as well. It's an Andalucian, summery version of ham and eggs!

Ingredients
Selection of summer leaves
Serrano ham (12 fine slices)
6 quails eggs
5 fresh figs
Chives (chopped and lengths)

Juice of I lemon
2 small red onions
70g white caster sugar
70ml white wine vinegar
Extra virgin olive oil
Freshly ground black pepper
Coarse sea salt

Wash and trim the leaves. Set aside in a large bowl, cover with a damp cloth then cling film and refrigerate. Finely slice the red onions. Put sugar and vinegar into a pan and place over low heat, add the sliced onions and bring to simmer. Continue simmering on a low heat for about 5 minutes, stir from time to time – the syrup should be pink and the onions soft. Strain the syrup and set aside to cool. Keep the onions (they go perfectly with cheese).

Place the quail's eggs into boiling water, add a dash of vinegar – this will help to remove the shell – and boil for 3 minutes. Run under cold water and peel. Cut each egg in half and sprinkle with a little sea salt and pepper. Set aside.

Trim the tops off the figs and cut into quarters lengthways. We leave the skins on as they come straight from our tree, clean and untouched, however, if you prefer, the skins can be carefully removed. Drizzle the red onion syrup generously over the figs..

Construct the salad using the leaves as a base. Loosely roll the Serrano ham and place in with the leaves. Sprinkle with chopped chives, season with pepper and drizzle with olive oil. Arrange the eggs and figs in the same way adding more leaves along the way distributing colours and textures evenly. Garnish with chives, drizzle generously with olive oil and lemon juice.

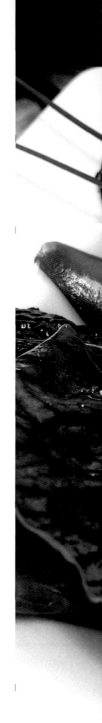

Fragrant rice salad with cardamom and coriander

Another simple, healthy dish that's easy to prepare in advance and good to eat in the summer. The vegetables are best hardly cooked.

4 cups of rice (any type)
1 small courgette
4 carrots
2 leeks
2 lengths of celery
1 large green pepper
1 teaspoon ground cardamom
1 teaspoon ground coriander
1 large lemon
1 generous bunch of fresh coriander
Extra virgin olive oil
Sea salt coarse
Freshly milled black pepper

Bring a large pan of water to boil. Add the rice and cook rapidly for about 7 minutes (or until just done). Remove from heat, strain and rinse with cold running water to remove the starch. When ready the water should run clear not cloudy. Set rice aside.

Peel the carrots, cut into fine strips and dice. Dice the courgette in a similar way. Trim the leeks, remove the outer layers, slice and finely dice. Finely chop the celery and the green pepper. Chop the coriander. Take a large pan and heat a small amount of olive oil. Add the diced vegetables and constantly stir over high heat for one minute. Remove from heat and stir into the dry, washed rice. Finely zest and juice the lemon and add to the rice. Add the fresh coriander and spices. Season to taste. Refrigerate until time to serve.

Serve as part of a variety of salads or with marinated salmon. Goes well with a chilled white wine on the fruity side.

Roasted quail, summer leaves, pine nuts with walnut oil and chutney

A time consuming dish but it makes a good first course for dinner or on its own as a light lunch. A medium white Muscatel from the Malaga region goes well.

4 whole quail
1 onion (sliced)
2 bay leaves
150g mixed leaves
1 dessert spoon fresh thyme
Small bunch chives
20g pine nuts

30ml walnut oil
30ml extra virgin olive oil
15ml balsamic vinegar
½ teaspoon grain mustard
100ml water
Freshly milled black pepper
Salt

To serve
4 dessertspoons apple and rosemary chutney p.242
4 sautéed rounds of bread

Pre heat the oven to 200°C. Line an oven proof dish with foil, place the onion slices on the bottom with the bay leaves. Place the quail on top and drizzle generously with olive oil. Sprinkle with thyme leaves, loosely cover (but do not seal) with more foil and bake for 20 minutes. Remove from the oven and leave to rest. Sauté the pine nuts in a little olive oil until just golden, remove quickly from the heat and turn out onto kitchen paper. Prepare the salad leaves. Chop the chives.

Remove the quail from the dish. With a sharp knife, remove the breasts and carefully cut off the legs. Set aside for the salad. Take the carcasses and place in a small pan with the water. Press the bones (squeeze with your hands) and mash into the water, add the onion and juices from the pan. Set on medium heat and simmer for 1 minute. Strain through a conical sieve, press hard to extract all the juices. Retain the liquid. To make the dressing mix the extracted liquid with the balsamic vinegar, mustard, walnut and olive oils, season well.

To serve, the salad is best laid up individually in shallow bowls. Lay one piece of sautéed bread in each bowl, place a spoon of chutney on top. On top of this, arrange two breasts and two legs, Drizzle with the dressing. Arrange the leaves, sprinkle with pine nuts and chives. Drizzle with olive oil and serve.

Bean sprouts, green pepper, mushroom, croutons

Raw bean sprouts have a unique flavour and always feel healthy to eat. They have similarities with the raw green pepper - the added texture and crunch of the croutons and the earthy, mellow flavour of the mushrooms go extremely well.

150g fresh bean sprouts
1 green pepper
6 small closed mushrooms
2 slices thick cut bread
½ white onion
1 clove garlic
100ml extra virgin olive oil
Sea salt
Freshly ground black pepper

Remove the crusts from the bread (they are not needed). Cut the slices into small cubes. Peel and finely chop the garlic. Put 1 tablespoon olive oil into a frying pan and heat. Sauté the garlic for about 1 minute. Remove from the pan and set aside. Add a little more oil and toss in the cubes of bread. Sauté, turning quickly until golden all over. Remove from the pan and turn out onto kitchen paper. Finely dice the onion, green pepper and mushrooms.

To construct the salad put the bean sprouts into a large bowl, add all the other ingredients, toss, season, drizzle with olive oil and serve.

Carpaccio of seared buey, rocket and manchego

This is our Spanish slant on the Italian classic. Buey (bull) has plenty of flavour and the Manchego puts up a good fight although it has a more rounded taste and is without the cutting edge of Parmesan.

250g buey fillet (or prime beef fillet)
150g baby rocket
120g mature Manchego cheese
1 white Spanish onion (mild)
20g pine nuts
Freshly milled black pepper(coarse)
Coarse sea salt
Extra virgin olive oil

Sauté the pine nuts for a few seconds in a little olive oil until just golden, quickly remove from the pan and turn out onto kitchen paper. Prepare the beef or buey fillet making sure it is free of fat and cylindrical in shape. Season generously with salt and pepper. Heat a little olive oil in a shallow pan and sear the fillet on high heat, turning quickly on all sides. Turn off the heat, and let the meat rest. Ultra-finely slice the onion. Ultra-finely slice the cheese and drizzle with olive oil. Finely slice the meat and drizzle with olive oil.

To construct the salad put the rocket into a large bowl, distribute the meat slices, cheese and onion. Drizzle with the meat juices and olive oil, sprinkle with pine nuts, season with black pepper. Serve immediately.

Marinated duck, spinach, orange, sesame and soy

This dish is a meal in itself and a favourite late-night snack. The duck partners the orange, the soy cuts the balsamic vinegar and the ginger adds tang. It can take a good peppery rocket.

1 duck breast
150g baby spinach leaves
50g rocket leaves
2 large oranges
1 scallion (spring onion)
1 fresh cooked beetroot
1 tablespoon sesame seeds
Fresh ginger root (4cm length)
50g caster sugar
50ml balsamic vinegar
50ml sesame oil
20ml 100% soy sauce
Extra virgin olive oil
Freshly ground black pepper
Salt

Heat 1 teaspoon of olive oil in a shallow pan. Season the duck breast, add to the pan (skin side down) and sear for 4 minutes. Reduce the heat, turn over carefully and sear the other side for a further 3 minutes. Remove the duck breast and put into a dish, pour over the juices and cover immediately with cling film.

Peel one of the oranges with a potato peeler, cut the peel into fine strips and set aside for garnish. To make the marinade, finely zest the other orange using a grater. Juice both oranges and put all into a small pan with the sugar. Peel and grate the ginger root, add to the pan and simmer for 1 minute over low heat. Remove, stir in the soy sauce, vinegar and sesame oil. Uncover the duck and slice thinly, spreading out the slices. Pour the marinade over and cover. Finely slice the scallion and finely dice the beetroot.

To construct the salad, put the spinach and rocket into a large bowl, toss in the scallions, orange strips and beetroot cubes. Layer in the duck slices, drizzle the salad with the marinade, season generously with pepper, sprinkle with sesame seeds and serve immediately.

Salad of parsley stalks, shredded carrots and new seasons garlic in mustard vinaigrette

In this salad the young parsley stalks are one of the main ingredients hence you need plenty of them – it's ideal if you grow your own or like here, you can buy them in huge bunches. You need to be selective using only the small tender stems.

Large handful of selected parsley stalks
3 medium carrots
Half a mild white onion
1 whole head of garlic
1 table spoon mustard (smooth)
100ml extra virgin olive oil
25ml white wine vinegar

Prepare the vegetables. Peel the garlic cloves. Peel the carrots and cut into fine sticks approximately 5cm long. Cut the parsley stalks to the same length. Fill a pan with water and bring to the boil. Blanch the carrots and parsley stalks for one minute. Remove and immediately immerse in cold water to prevent further cooking. Drain and set aside. Put 1 tablespoon of olive oil into a pan and gently sauté the garlic cloves for about 3 minutes until slightly golden. Add 2 tablespoons water and leave to simmer until the water has evaporated. Turn off the heat and leave covered for 5 minutes. The garlic will be cooked but will taste fresh rather than roasted.

Mix the mustard, olive oil and vinegar together in a large bowl. Finely dice the onion and add to the bowl. Add the vegetables, toss carefully and turn out into a serving dish. Season with pepper.

Serve on its own with fresh bread or as a light healthy accompaniment to a grilled steak.

Salad of fresh cheese, mango and rocket with citrus infusion

Mangos grow in a protected valley in their own microclimate just south of us. The Muscatel grapes grow alongside - they are laid out to dry in neat beds as has been done for hundreds of years. The cheese is made on the top of the hill overlooking the valley.

1 large mango ripe but firm
100g fresh cheese (cow or sheep milk)
100g rocket leaves
100g Malaga seedless raisins (or large sultanas)
½ small red pepper
1 green leek top
White sesame seeds
Freshly milled black pepper
Sea salt
Extra virgin olive oil
1 lime
1 lemon
1 orange
2 tablespoons caster sugar
1 teaspoon white wine vinegar

Finely zest and juice the lime, lemon and orange. Put all this in a pan, add the sugar and vinegar and leave to infuse. Meanwhile remove the skin from the mango, cut down around the pip to remove the two main halves of flesh and set these aside for the salad. Scrape the remaining flesh from the sides of the pip, mash its juice into a bowl and add this to the citrus infusion. Put the pan on the heat and bring to a gentle simmer, stir constantly until the sugar has dissolved. Remove and leave to cool. Cut the fresh cheese into fine slices and place on a large plate, drizzle generously with olive oil and season well. Strain the citrus infusion, retaining the liquid for drizzling. Cut the mango flesh into slices, spread out on a large plate and drizzle with a little citrus infusion. Finely slice the inner bright green top of the leek. Finely dice the red pepper. Roughly chop the raisins. Prepare the rocket removing any 'stalky' stems.

Construct the salad layering the mango, cheese and rocket leaves. Scatter the leek strips, raisins and red pepper. Drizzle with the remaining citrus infusion and olive oil. Sprinkle sparingly with sesame seeds. Serve immediately.

Salad of langoustines, chicory and orange

Langoustines are available everywhere in this region, they are synonomous with the summer, the sun and the sea. The region is also famous for its sweet winter oranges. This salad combines these delicous fresh tasting flavours and goes particularly well with a chilled white Albariño from Galicia.

1 kilo large langoustines (cooked)	2 tablespoons caster sugar
4 chicory heads	Fresh root ginger (4 cm length)
1 frisée lettuce	2 cloves garlic (peeled)
4 sweet oranges	1 dessertspoon smooth mustard
2 scallions (spring onions)	3 tablespoons natural mayonnaise p.241
200ml extra virgin olive oil	1 bunch of fresh coriander
1 tablespoon white wine vinegar	Small sprigs of fresh dill and chives
2 lemons	Salt and freshly ground black pepper

Remove the heads and tails from the langoustines. Peel off the shell starting from the underneath side between the legs. Remove the waste vein and rinse under cold water. Rest on ice untll job complete. Pat dry, cover and refrigerate.

To make the dressing, zest and juice one orange and both the lemons. Put the juice into the small pan, add the sugar and gently heat until dissolved. Mix the olive oil, vinegar and mustard in a large bowl. Finely grate the garlic and the ginger. Add to the dressing and season well. Set aside some coriander sprigs, dill and long chives for garnish. Finely chop the remaining herbs, add to the dressing. Finally add the mayonnaise, mix thoroughly. and season.

Prepare the oranges. Remove the skin and pith. Cut into small segments. Finely chop the spring onion. Prepare the chicory and frisée.

Plate up or arrange in one large dish. Start with a base of mixed leaves, then some prawns, orange segments and spring onion. Pour over some dressing. Layer again. Garnish with coriander, dill and long chives. Serve immediately.

Pear, watercress and strawberry salad with grain mustard dressing

This is a very feminine salad where the pear's delicate fragrance is contrasted by the gentle heat of the watercress, the sweetness of the strawberry and a hint of texture in the mustard.

2 bunches watercress
4 large ripe strawberries
3 large ripe pears
100ml extra virgin olive oil
1 tablespoon grain mustard
1 tablespoon white wine vinegar
50g caster sugar
50ml water
1 lemon
Salt
Freshly milled pepper

Finely zest and juice the lemon. Put into a small pan on low heat. Add the water and sugar, leave to dissolve. Peel the pears and put the skin into the pan. Mash into the liquid and simmer for 2 minutes. Strain through a conical sieve retaining the liquid. Cut the pear flesh into oval shapes, put in a bowl and pour the liquid over them. To make the vinaigrette, mix the grain mustard, vinegar and olive oil, season with salt and pepper. Trim the watercress. Trim the strawberry tops and slice. Construct the salad carefully tossing all the ingredients together. Drizzle with the vinaigrette and the sweet pear juices. Serve immediately.

Spinach, feta cheese, peppers and sunflower seeds

This is another one of those favourite salads which is a meal in itself and can be eaten at any time of day. The flavourful feta adds just the right amount of saltiness against the sweet raisins. The tiny diced raw vegetables are typically Andalucian being the garnish for the famous 'Gazpacho'.

1 red pepper
1 green pepper
½ cucumber
1 small red onion
2 vine tomatoes (not too ripe)
100g baby spinach leaves
100g feta cheese
50g seedless Malaga raisins (or sultanas)
1 tablespoon sunflower seeds
100ml extra virgin olive oil
20ml white wine vinegar
Juice from 1 large lemon
Freshly ground black pepper

De-seed the peppers, cut into thin strips and finely dice. Place in large salad bowl. Peel the cucumber and onion, finely dice, season with a little pepper, add to bowl. Cut down the sides of the tomato and dice the flesh (including the skin), add to the bowl. Carefully cut the cheese into small cubes, roughly chop the raisins and add to the bowl. To make the vinaigrette, take the remaining tomato cores and squeeze their juices into a separate bowl. Add the olive oil, vinegar and lemon juice, season with pepper.

To serve, very gently mix the salad, add the baby spinach leaves, drizzle with the vinaigrette and sprinkle with sunflower seeds. Serve immediately.

Contents

soups

Fragrant langoustine broth with dumplings

We have been making this for a long time ever since discovering Asian ingredients. Not always easy to find in this part of the world but fresh lime leaves, lemon grass and galangal will all freeze if necessary.

2 litres light chicken broth see p.246
1 chicken breast
500g langoustines cooked
1 scallion
1 lime
1 bunch fresh basil (6 stalks)
1 bunch fresh coriander (12 stalks)
3 stalks whole fresh lemon grass
1 piece fresh galangal root 10cm length
1 piece ginger root 10cm length
6 fresh Kaffir lime leaves (if available)
200ml coconut milk

Finely slice the scallion, lemon grass, basil and coriander (reserve a few sprigs for the garnish). Finely grate the ginger and galangal. Zest and juice the lime.

Put aside 4 or 8 langoustines for the garnish. Peel the rest, remove the waste, rinse with water and dab dry. Cut the chicken up into pieces. Put into the food processor with half the peeled and cleaned langoustines. Add a heaped teaspoon of each of the following ingredients, scallions, basil, coriander and ginger. Pulse until smooth. Remove the paste and mould into small dumplings. Put the stock into a large pan and bring to the boil. Add all the prepared ingredients (except the coconut milk). Add the chicken dumplings and simmer gently for 30 minutes. Add the coconut milk and remaining langoustines. Take out the lime leaves.Serve hot with garnish.

Tomato soup with lemon balm and basil pesto

We make this fresh tasting soup in the summer when there are masses of tomatoes. It is good with or without the pesto.

1 kilo ripe vine tomatoes	**For the pesto**
1 medium onion	30 basil leaves (about 20g)
2 oranges	Fine zest from 1 small lemon
1 lemon	2 tablespoons pine kernels
2 teaspoons caster sugar	30g medium Manchego cheese
10 basil leaves	Freshly ground black pepper
1 drop lemon balm essential oil	Pinch of salt
1 tablespoon extra virgin olive oil	
Freshly ground black pepper	

Roughly chop the onion. Put in a large stainless steel pan, sauté on low heat in olive oil to soften (do not brown). Roughly chop the tomatoes, collect the juices and add all to the pan. Juice the oranges, add to the pan. Finely zest and juice the lemon, add to the pan. Add the basil leaves, sugar and season with black pepper. Bring quickly to simmer, cover, turn down the heat and cook on low for 7 minutes. Cool a little, pour into a blender, add the lemon balm oil carefully with a pipette and liquidize. Strain through a conical sieve. Pour the soup back into the pan. Leave to sit for at least 30 minutes.

To make the pesto. Finely chop the basil. Finely grate the cheese. Finely chop the pine nuts. Combine all the ingredients to make a rough herb paste. Season with black pepper and salt to taste.

Note. You can use fresh lemon balm if you have it - roughly chop a good handful of leaves and put them in with the tomatoes to blend - it tastes good but does change the colour of the soup.

To serve, warm the soup very gently, spoon the pesto on top.

Garlic and almond soup with sweet pea puree

A hot version of the delicious 'Ajo blanco'. This is made with chicken stock and therefore has more depth and body. It makes a good Spring soup when the weather is neither hot nor cold.

200g whole almonds
6 garlic cloves
2 med white onions
100g peas or mange tout
1 large apple
1 dessertspoon caster sugar
1 sprig thyme
1 bay leaf
Freshly ground black pepper
1 litre light chicken stock p.246
100ml extra virgin olive oil
50ml double cream

To make the soup. Finely chop the onions and the garlic and sauté in olive oil over low heat until tender (do not brown). Add the chicken stock and bring to simmer. Put the almonds in the food processor or blender and grind to a rough powder, Add to the stock and simmer for 10 minutes. Remove from heat and cool slightly. Put the soup back into the processor, season with black pepper and blend until smooth. Stir in the double cream.

To prepare the purée. Peel the apple, dice the flesh and put into a small pan with 200ml water. Add the thyme and bay leaf. Simmer gently until the flesh is soft. Add the sugar and continue to cook for 1 minute. Leave to cool slightly, remove the thyme and bay leaf, pour all into the blender. Bring a larger pan of water to boil. Blanch the peas or mange tout for about 2 minutes. Drain and put into the blender. Blend the peas and the apple liquid to a fine puree, season with black pepper.

To serve, warm the soup over low heat, pour into bowls, add a tablespoon of purée to the centre of each bowl.

Cream of celeriac soup

A winter favourite that we often serve at Christmas.

1 celeriac head
2 white onions
1 apple
1 clove garlic
300ml cream
Sea salt
Freshly milled black pepper

For the vegetable stock
1 white onion
2 sticks celery
6 mushrooms
3 fresh bay leaves
1 teaspoon peppercorns
1 sprig fresh thyme
1 bunch ripped parsley
1.5l water
Extra virgin olive oil

Prepare the stock
Roughly chop the celery, onion and mushrooms, Place in a large sauce pan and sauté in a little olive oil on medium heat until starting to colour. Add the water, thyme, peppercorns and parsley. Simmer for 30 minutes. Strain, retaining the liquor and pour back into the pan.

Peel and cut the celeriac into cubes. Slice the onion, peel and dice the apple, finely chop the garlic. Put all into the pan. Simmer for 30 minutes. Leave to cool slightly. Put all in the blender and blend until smooth. Add 250ml cream and blend. Serve hot.

Light chicken broth with saffron, scallions and dim sum dumplings

Memories of China town occasionally cooked here in Andalucia.

1 litre light chicken stock p.246
3 scallions (spring onions)
Fresh ginger root (3cm length)
Sea salt
1g saffron

For the dumplings
1 pack wonton wrappers (rice skins)
200g pork loin
½ small onion
1 garlic clove
Fresh ginger root (3cm length)
1 egg yolk
Pinch dried oregano or thyme
Freshly ground black pepper
1 whole egg mixed to glaze

Prepare the dumplings
Cut the pork into chunks. Finely dice the onion and garlic. Peel and finely grate the ginger. Put the pork, onion, garlic, egg yolk, ginger, herbs and seasoning into the food processor and grind to a paste. Take the wrappers and soften in warm water for about 30 seconds. Drain on kitchen paper. Place a small quantity of pork paste in the centre of each wrapper and brush the edges lightly with egg mix. Fold the wrapper edges up over the filling and seal (fold under or twist to make a pouch). Brush the base of a bamboo steam basket with a little oil (if you don't have one, a stainless steel colander will do). Place the dumplings on the basket and steam over a large pan of boiling water for about 10 minutes. Do not let the water touch the bottom of the steamer.

Heat the chicken stock in a large pan. Finely slice the scallions and add to the pan. Peel and finely grate the ginger, add to the pan. Add the saffron, season and gently simmer for a few minutes. Add the pre-cooked dumplings. Serve hot.

Beetroot soup with sour cream and dill

This is a velvety and very flavourfull soup. Adaptable to serve warm in the winter with its spicy, festive overtones or on ice, chilled in glasses on a hot summer night.

2 large beetroot
2 red onions
4 large oranges
2 star anise
2 cloves
1 small bay leaf
1 cinnamon stick
100ml red wine
400ml water
2 tablespoons extra virgin olive oil
Small bunch dill
Freshly ground pepper
30ml thick crème fraiche or soured cream

Finely chop the red onions. Finely zest 2 oranges. Juice all 4 oranges. Peel the beetroot and dice into 1cm cubes. In a medium pan put the red wine, orange juice, beetroot cubes, bay leaf, cloves, cinnamon and star anise. Heat over low heat for a few minutes. Add the water and orange zest, cover and simmer gently for 20 minutes. Meanwhile gently sauté the onions in the olive oil (do not brown). Finely chop a few sprigs of dill. When the beetroot is done remove the spices and bay leaf from the liquor. Put the cooked beetroot, the liquor, cooked onions and dill into the blender, season generously with pepper, Blend thoroughly until very smooth. Test the consistency, adding a little water if necessary.

Serve hot or cold with sour cream and sprigs of dill.

Strawberry gazpacho

We always make this refreshing soup in early summer as the weather heats up. It is lighter and more fragrant than the traditional version.

250g fresh ripe strawberries (approx 16)
4 medium vine tomatoes
1 large red pepper
3 cloves peeled garlic
1 lemon
1 large orange
1 medium mild white onion

Dice the tomatoes, onion and pepper. De stalk the strawberries and cut in half. Zest and juice the orange and lemon. Liquidize all the ingredients thoroughly. Strain through a conical sieve, cover and refrigerate. Serve cold with crushed ice.

Contents

seafood

Carpaccio tuna, marinated plums, vodka red onions and ginger

This is a more unusual alternative to the classic salmon carpaccio. We use extremely fresh Mediterranean tuna and prefer to use fish that are pale in colour for this dish. The raw flesh tastes fresher and is more subtle and less 'bloody' than the dark red variety.

400g tuna loin (one piece, no skin, no bones)
½ large red onion
4 red plums (firm but ripe)
Fresh ginger root (3 cm length)
30ml vodka
Juice from 1 lime
1 tablespoon caster sugar
100ml extra virgin olive oil
Freshly ground black pepper
Sea salt flakes

Prepare the fresh tuna, cut into two neat, clean pieces. Wrap each tightly in cling film and put in the freezer to chill for a hour or so. Ultra-finely slice the red onion, put in a small pan with the vodka, cover and heat gently to simmer for 1 minute (the onions should be still slightly crunchy but not too strong). Set aside for serving.

Carefully peel the plums with a very sharp knife. Cut the peel into fine strips to garnish. Cut down either side of the stone. Set aside the stone part (and the small amount of flesh attached). Finely slice the plum halves and spread out in a shallow dish. Put the stone pieces into a small pan with enough water to cover (about 150ml). Peel and finely grate the ginger, add to the pan, cover and cook for 5 minutes. Stir in the sugar, cook for 1 more minute. Remove from heat and press through a conical sieve. Retain the resulting sludge, put into a small bowl. Stir in the lime juice and 50ml olive oil, pour over the plums.

To serve, finely slice the chilled tuna with a very sharp knife and arrange on plates. Spoon on the marinated plums and the marinade. Scatter the onions and the plum skin strips. Drizzle with olive oil, season with salt flakes and pepper, eat immediately.

Seared scallops, tempura leeks, carrot and cumin purée

This dish makes a good first course. It's a very textural dish with the crisp leeks and the sweet aromatic carrot contrasting the soft, buttery scallops.

12 fresh scallops in their shells	6 carrots
Extra virgin olive oil	1 bay leaf
Little unsalted butter	1 teaspoon cumin seeds
	1 clove garlic (cut in half)
1 leek	25g unsalted butter
1 egg white	1 tablespoon double cream
3 tablespoon corn flour	Sea salt
1 tablespoon cold water	Freshly ground black pepper

To prepare the scallops, remove them from their shells. Remove waste, trim, rinse and dry carefully.

For the carrot purée, put a medium pan of water on to boil, add the bay leaf, half the cumin seeds and the garlic. Peel and finely dice the carrots. Boil until tender. Drain, Keep the carrots and the liquor. Put the carrots in the blender and pulp. Add the remaining cumin seeds, butter and cream. Season generously with pepper. Blend again. Add the liquor a little at a time until you have a perfectly smooth purée.

For the tempura leeks, trim and remove the outer layer of leek. Cut in half and finely slice. Put the egg white, water and corn flour into a bowl, mix well. Dip the leek strips into the batter and drop, a few at a time, into hot oil to fry. Set aside to drain on kitchen paper, season sparingly with salt.

To prepare for serving, spoon the purée in a curved line onto the plates.

To cook the scallops, sauté in a little olive oil and butter over medium heat for 2 minutes each side until lightly golden. Add the cream to the pan, season and leave to stand for 1 minute,

To serve, place the scallops in the centre of the plate, spoon over the creamed juices, garnish with the leeks.

Octopus with crushed raspberries, green herb oil

A cleansing little plate of wow!

250g octopus cooked and sliced
½ small red onion (chopped)
100g fresh raspberries
1 lime juiced
50ml raspberry vinegar
50g caster sugar
1 bunch fresh dill
Extra virgin olive oil
Salt and freshly ground black pepper

Put half the raspberries into a small pan with the sugar, vinegar and onion. Put on low heat, simmer gently for 7 minutes. Strain through a conical sieve. Set aside the liquid. Crush the rest of the raspberries, set aside and drizzle with lime juice. Finely chop the dill, put in the blender with 150ml olive oil. Blend until smooth, strain. Retain the oil.

To serve, drizzle the serving plate with raspberry syrup and green oil. Place the octopus slices on top, add the mashed raspberries and more green oil. Serve immediately.

Fish terrine

350g prepared salmon	250g prepared white fish meat
½ red onion	2 green scallion tops
1 lemon	70ml double cream
70ml double cream	
2 large leeks	Sea salt
Spinach leaves	Freshly ground black pepper
Extra virgin olive oil	Cling film

To achieve the pink and green layers you need to prepare two coloured fish pastes. For the pink paste, you will need prepared salmon – without skin or bones. Cut a few slices approx 100g – enough to make a layer in the terrine. Cut the rest into rough chunks. Finely zest and juice the lemon. Finely chop the red onion. Put in the food processor with the fish chunks, season well and blend on high for 30 seconds. Scrape down the sides of the mixer to make sure that all the paste is well blended and pulse again. Spoon the paste out and set aside. For the green fish paste, finely chop the spring onion tops and the herbs. Roughly cut the white fish into small pieces and put in the food processor. Add the onions, herbs, cream and season well. Blend until smooth.
Put a large, wide pan of water on to boil (you will need this later – it needs to be about 20cm in diameter but not necessarily deep). Trim the leeks, remove the outer layer. Separate the layers and blanch in the water for 2 minutes. Remove, drain and dab dry with kitchen paper. (You will need about 10 layers of leek for the outside, the rest makes a layer in the terrine). Wilt the spinach in pan with a little olive oil, season well.

Pre heat the oven to 220°C. To construct the terrine. Lay two layers of cling film into the terrine, overlapping the edges by 10cm all round. Put in the leek strips (running front to back), until you have a green leek lined terrine. Place the salmon slices on the bottom. Spread the pink fish paste evenly over. Make a layer of spinach, more pink fish paste, a layer of leeks, a layer of green fish paste. Layer the top with leeks, wrap up the edges of the cling film. Place the terrine in an oven proof dish. It needs to have space all round and deep enough to hold water to half way up the terrine sides – pour the water in and cover the entire thing with foil. Bake in the oven for 40 minutes. Remove and leave to cool for 20 minutes. You now need to find a way to press down on the terrine for at least 6 hours in the refrigerator. Full juice or milk cartons work well. The better pressed, the better the terrine will hold together.

To serve, use a very sharp knife to cut into thick slices, serve with its own jelly and dill pickle (substitute apple for gherkin) see p.243.

Langoustines with lemon, garlic mayonnaise

Fresh langoustines are easy to buy here with some of the best found in markets along the coast – they must be absolutely fresh and cooked on the day of purchase. In the heat, keep on ice in a cool box for the journey home.

1 kilo fresh langoustines
2 lemons

Bring a large pan of water to boil. Drop in the langoustines and cook rapidly for 2 minutes. Remove quickly and plunge immediately into a tub filled with iced water. Add more ice to keep cool. Refrigerate for 30 minutes, Serve whole with lemon quarters, garlic mayonnaise and country bread.

For the garlic mayonnaise
1 free range egg
¼ teaspoon smooth French mustard
2 teaspoons caster sugar
Pinch salt
2 tablespoons white wine vinegar
4 cloves garlic
500ml extra virgin olive oil

Finely grate the garlic. Put the egg, mustard, sugar, salt, vinegar and garlic into the blender. Blend a little. Whilst still blending, slowly pour in the oil (through the hole at the top of the blender), keep a steady stream. As the mixture starts to emulsify, increase the speed. When fully blended serve as an accompaniment to the fish.

Seared langoustines, garlic, wilted radicchio and orange dressing

A tasty dish that makes a good winter first course.

1 kilo cooked langoustines
6 cloves garlic
1 red radicchio
1 red onion
1 large sweet orange
1 tablespoon caster sugar
2 teaspoons orange vinegar
Extra virgin olive oil

Pinch the heads and tails off the langoustines. Peel off the skins (pull apart from the centre underneath). Discard for this recipe but they make a great broth. Using a small knife cut down the backs and remove the waste tracts. Wash and pat dry.

Peel and finely slice the garlic. Finely zest and juice the orange. Put the juice into a small pan with the sugar and heat to a light syrup. Remove the outer layer of the radicchio and separate the leaves. Finely slice the red onion. Heat a little olive oil in a large shallow pan and wilt the radicchio leaves on medium heat. Turn out onto a serving plate. Season with black pepper. Sauté the onions until golden and crisp, turn out and set aside. Put the langoustines into the pan, add a little more oil and sauté for 30 seconds, Turn over, add the garlic to the pan and continue cooking for another 30 seconds. Add the orange vinegar, orange zest and syrup, reduce for a few seconds, take off the heat and cover for one minute. Turn out onto the radicchio and drizzle with olive oil. Garnish with the onions and serve.

Lobster, endive, tomato and rosemary dressing

We don't serve this dish very often but when we do it's on request for the whole table. The restaurant goes silent and everyone wants one. Here is just one way to cook lobsters and we like to serve them simply.

2 live lobsters about 1 kilo each
3 endive pale green heads
3 vine tomatoes
2 sprigs fresh rosemary
Juice from one lemon
30ml white wine vinegar
70ml extra virgin olive oil
1 teaspoon smooth mustard
2 teaspoons caster sugar
Sea salt (plenty for water during cooking)
Freshly ground black pepper

Fill a very large pan with water (about two thirds full). Add 2 tablespoons sea salt for each litre of water. Bring the water to a vigorous boil over high heat. Place the live lobsters into the water quickly, one at a time, headfirst, completely submerging them. Pick up the lobsters by holding the upper side of the thorax between your thumb and middle finger. Cover the pot tightly and return to the boil rapidly. When the water is back to boiling point start timing the cooking. Your 1 kilo lobsters will need about 12 minutes cooking (continuous vigorous boiling). They will turn bright red in colour. When the time is up, pull the lobsters out and immediately plunge into a tub of iced cold water. When cool, dab dry and refrigerate for 30 minutes.

Cut the outer layer from the endive bulbs and separate the leaves, arrange on a serving platter. Finely dice the tomatoes, season with salt and drizzle generously with olive oil, scatter over the endive. To make the dressing put the sugar, lemon juice and vinegar into a small pan and place over low heat until the sugar has dissolved. Add 1 teaspoon finely chopped rosemary, remove from the heat and leave to infuse for 5 minutes. Stir in the mustard and olive oil, Cool and pour over the salad. Scatter more rosemary leaves to finish.

To serve cut open the lobster tail and crack open the claws - carefully remove the meat. Arrange with the salad. Serve with mayonnaise p.241 and rustic bread.

Fish baked in sea salt

This is one of the most perfect ways of eating fish. It is messy to serve and is quite a skill to master but the reward of eating it is more than worth it.

Whole fish sea bream
Coarse sea salt
Bay leaves
Sprigs fresh thyme
Lemon (cut into quarters)
Onion (cut into quarters)

Boiled new potatoes
Parsley and lemon
Green salad leaves
Extra virgin olive oil

When selecting the fish allow 500g whole weight per person minimum. The bigger the fish the better. You will need approximately the same amount of salt. A two kilo fish needs 2 kilos of salt. Get the fishmonger to clean.

Pre heat the oven to 200°C. Choose an oven proof dish big enough to hold the fish with space all around. Spread a layer of salt over the bottom. Place the lemon, onion, bay and thyme in the cavity. Wet the skin of the fish with a little water, place on the salt. Cover the entire fish with more salt. Wet the salt with a little water. Place in the centre of a hot oven. Allow 30 minutes cooking time per kilo.

To serve, crack open the salt (which will harden in the oven) – use the top side of a heavy knife. Carefully pull the salt off the fish – the skin should pull away with the salt. Push any loose salt away with a spoon and a brush. Carefully lift the flesh off the bone and place onto warm serving plates. Pull the main bone up and lift the rest of the fish onto the plate. Drizzle with olive oil. Serve with boiled new potatoes, chopped parsley, olive oil and lemon.

Note. Many people argue that leaving the fish scales on and or adding egg whites to the salt can help the salt to crust better. Howerver, there is an art to serving this dish! It can be perfected with practice. The difficulty is to, a) to remove the salt without 'salting' the fish, b) to remove the flesh without it breaking up too much and finally, c) to serve it whilst still hot!

Contents

main course

Pork fillet with glazed apple, thyme, black pudding stuffing and wild mushrooms

Pork is very popular all over Spain and in Andalucia the Morcilla or black pudding is prized - with butchers all making their own specialities. It pairs particularly well with the green cabbage and this in turn goes well with apple and thyme.

600g pork fillet or loin (no fat)
1 onion
Sprig thyme

1 teaspoon thyme leaves
2 apples
1 small lemon juiced
1 tablespoon caster sugar

For the black pudding stuffing
1 morcilla (black pudding) 350g
140g pork fillet or loin (no fat)
4 cloves garlic
1 red onion
1 teaspoon dried oregano
1 egg yolk
30g white breadcrumbs
1 green cabbage
2 bay leaves

200g wild mushrooms such as
chanterelle
Salt
Freshly ground black pepper
Extra virgin olive oil

1.5kilo peeled potatoes
50ml double cream
70g mild hard cheese

Cling film
Elastic bands

To prepare the black pudding stuffing.
Peel and finely chop the onion and garlic. Put in a pan with 1 tablespoon olive oil, cover and sauté for 3 minutes until soft and slightly coloured. Remove the skin from the black pudding, cut the pudding into pieces. Cut the pork into pieces. Put the pudding, pork, egg yolk, oregano, breadcrumbs and contents of pan into the food processor. Blend a little (it should be well mixed but not over blended). Remove the pudding paste, set aside.

Put a large pan of water on to boil. Select the best green cabbage leaves (about 10) cut in half, removing the hard central spine. Add the bay leaves to the water. Blanch the leaves in boiling water for 3-4 minutes, remove the leaves and set aside on a kitchen towel to dry. Retain the pan of water. Place 3 layers of cling film on the work surface (approximately 40cm x 40cm). Place the cabbage leaves on this about 10cm in from the edges of the film. Run front to back, layering to make a green cabbage square about 20cm x 20cm. Take the black pudding paste and mould it into a fat sausage shape with your hands, its length should be about 20cm.

Place it along the front edge of the cabbage. Take the front edges of the cling film and roll the pudding up in the cabbage, fold over the cling film and twist both ends.

You should now have a cling filmed cabbage-covered sausage. Wrap in one last long layer of cling film. Twist and tie the ends firmly with elastic bands, keep twisting as you do this to tighten the sausage. Put the water back on to boil. Drop the sausage into the water and poach (gentle simmer with lid on) for 30 minutes. Take out and leave to sit for 5 minutes. Put in a dish, snip the cling film and catch the juices, unwrap. Leave the sausage in the dish with juices, cover the dish with cling film.

To make the layered potatoes
Pre heat the oven to 220°C. Peel and slice the potatoes. Put in a large pan of boiling water to par boil. The potatoes should be just soft, drain and put in large bowl. Season well, stir in the cream and cheese. Tip out into an oven proof dish and bake for 30 minutes until golden, remove and leave to cool slightly.

To cook the pork
Roughly chop the onion. Line an oven tray with foil and spread the onion over the bottom. Drizzle generously with olive oil. Season the pork well, (if you have a loin cut it lengthways into two long sections), place on top, add the sprig of thyme and 1 tablespoon olive oil. Draw up the edges of the foil to make a parcel. Seal and cook in the oven for 20 minutes. Remove and leave to stand.

For the accompanying vegetables
Dry clean the mushrooms carefully and sauté in a little olive oil. Season and set aside. Peel and finely dice the apple. Put in a large shallow pan with 1 tablespoon olive oil, cover and sauté on low heat until tender (about 3 minutes). Uncover, add the sugar, lemon juice and thyme, continue to cook for 30 seconds, turn out and set aside.

To serve.
Warm the plates. Drain the juices from the apple, the pork and the stuffed cabbage. Put into a shallow pan and heat to simmer, strain. Position a cube of potato and a slice of stuffed cabbage near the centre of each plate. Carve the pork fillet, place to the side, scatter the glazed apple, wild mushrooms and thyme, spoon over the strained juices and drizzle with olive oil. Serve immediately.

Grilled sea bass, fennel risotto, wild mushrooms

Spring arrives early and we pick the tender, sweet wild fennel shoots. Alongside, through the damp leaves come the wild mushrooms. We like to keep fish 'clean' and simply cooked, this fresh tasting green risotto is a perfect accompaniment.

2 Sea bass (each 1.5 kilo, cleaned and scaled)

For the stock
2 fresh bay leaves
1 stalk fresh rosemary
1 stalk (celery roughly chopped)
2 onions (roughly chopped)
1 dessertspoon peppercorns

Bunch wild fennel shoots
200g fresh baby spinach
100g wild mushrooms
(any local variety - chanterelle,
 trompette de mort, boletus)

Extra virgin olive oil (plenty)
Sea salt
Frshly ground black pepper

For the risotto
1 white onion
1 stalk celery
1 Fennel bulb (halved)
3 closed cap button mushrooms
1 bay leaf
1 clove garlic
1 lemon
Fresh parsley
250g short grain rice
30ml anise seco (dry)

To prepare the fish.
Cut off the heads and tails, discard, Remove the fillets. Set aside the bones for stock. Remove any small bones from the fillet with tweezers, trim leaving the skin on, cover and refrigerate for cooking later.

To prepare the stock for cooking the rice
Put the fish bones in a large pan with just over 1 litre of water. Add the bay leaves, peppercorns, rosemary, celery and onion. Bring to the boil and simmer for 25 minutes. Strain, retain the stock – you should have about 500ml.

139

To prepare the vegetables for the risotto

Finely chop the other half of the fennel bulb, the onions, mushrooms, celery and garlic. Put the pan back on the heat, add 1 tablespoon olive oil and a bay leaf, sauté the chopped vegetables on low heat until soft – do not brown. Remove from the heat. Ultra-finely chop the parsley. Finely zest the lemon. Add these to the pan, set aside and cover.

To make the risotto.

We prefer to add the prepared vegetables after cooking the rice – though this is unorthodox the dish retains a fresher taste. If you don't have anise you could substitute dry white wine or vermouth. Have the retained stock to hand. Put a large pan on the heat, add 2 tablespoons olive oil. When hot, tip in the rice, sauté for 1 minute, stir constantly, it will start to turn translucent. Add the anise, stir until absorbed (about 30 seconds). Add 400ml stock, turn the heat down and simmer gently, stir regularly and cook for 10 minutes. Add a little more stock as required to cook. It should take approx 12 minutes and 450ml stock to cook the rice to a creamy, 'just done' consistency. You will need to stir constantly towards the end to prevent sticking. Remove from the heat, stir in the prepared cooked vegetables, season generously with salt and pepper, cover and leave to sit.

For the accompanying vegetables

Dry clean the mushrooms carefully. Cut the remaining half a fennel bulb into oval shapes and sauté in a little olive oil on low heat until tender, If you have the wild shoots, add them to the pan, cook for 2 minutes. Tip out and set aside. Put the mushrooms in the pan, sauté on medium heat. Season, tip out and set aside. Put the spinach leaves in the pan, drizzle with olive oil and cover for 30 seconds to wilt - stir and cook for a few seconds more. Set aside.

To serve

Lightly oil the fillets, pan fry, skin side down in hot oil for 2 minutes, finish under a hot grill until just done. Drizzle with olive oil, lemon juice and black pepper. Serve with the rice and accompanying vegetables.

Seared tuna, capers, olives, tomatoes, garlic and polenta

This earthy dish mixes 'la huerta' - the kitchen garden, countryside and sea with most of the ingredients being served very nearly raw. From the garlic to the hillside capers, it's powerful and flavourful of earth and sea alike.

450g red tuna (no bones, no skin)
250g polenta (coarse yellow corn meal)

100g small caper berries
4 vine tomatoes
100g waxy black olives
3 cloves garlic
2 lemons
Parsley

1 teaspoon black sesame seeds
Extra virgin olive oil (plenty)
Sea salt flakes
Freshly ground black pepper

For the tomato reduction
1 large tomato
6 basil leaves (ripped)
2 tablespoons sugar
1 tablespoon white wine vinegar

To prepare the fish
For this dish we choose tuna with a deep red colour for its flavour. Make sure you buy a good sized piece - one from a quarter section of a large fish is good. Trim any blood-black flesh away and cut your piece into 2 approximate cylinder shapes as near to 6cm in diameter x 10cm long as you can.

To prepare the tomato reduction
Roughly dice the tomato. Put in a pan with the sugar, vinegar and basil. Bring to the boil and simmer for 3 minutes. Strain, pushing firmly down, set the reduction aside. If you like a strong basil flavour then you could simply liquidize rather than strain.

To cook the polenta
Put 250ml water into a pan with the polenta and heat, stir constantly until thick, (it can bubble up and spit – use a whisk and work fast) add 2 tablespoons olive oil and season generously with black pepper. If it gets too solid add a little more water. When done it should be a thick paste. Spoon out into a small square or rectangular container, approx 10cm x 10cm. Set aside to cool. Cut into 4 squares.

For the accompanying vegetables
Ultra finely chop the garlic and put in a medium sized bowl. Drain the caper berries (usually found in jars, in brine). Pit the olives and cut into quarters. Mix together with the garlic, add a little oil and set aside. Finely dice the tomatoes, put into a separate bowl with all their juices, sprinkle with a little salt and drizzle with olive oil. Juice the lemon, finely chop the parsley and add both to the tomatoes.

To serve.
Shallow fry the polenta on medium heat until golden and crispy on both sides, keep warm. Season the tuna generously on all sides, Sauté in olive oil on medium heat for 30 seconds – 2 minutes each side according to how rare you like it. Leave to sit and keep warm for 2 minutes. To serve, cut the tuna into thick slices, plate up on top of the polenta, dress with the tomatoes, capers and olives, drizzle with the tomato reduction and olive oil. Finally season the cut tuna with flaked sea salt, sprinkle with sesame seeds. Serve immediately.

Salmon trout with andaluz rice, clams

This is an entirely earthy dish – summing up one aspect of Andalucia in a mouthful. The trout are local and naturally farmed near Granada. We take some of the starch out of the rice during its preparation to allow the robust flavours of the garlic, saffron, pimento and woody herbs to retain their strength when served at table.

2 large whole salmon trout (each 1.5K cleaned)
500g clams (fresh in their shells)

For the andaluz rice
250g short grain rice
2 fresh bay leaves
1 tablespoon fresh rosemary leaves
1g saffron
2 cloves garlic
1 teaspoon fresh thyme leaves
1 stalk celery
1 white onion
1 green pepper
1 red pepper (small)
1 leek
1 lemon
1 teaspoon dried pimiento pepper

Extra virgin olive oil (plenty)
Salt
Freshly ground black pepper

For the fish stock
2 fresh bay leaves
1 stalk fresh rosemary
1 stalk celery (roughly chopped)
2 onions (roughly chopped)
1 dessertspoon peppercorns

For the sauce
2 shallots
1 garlic clove
1 bay leaf
8 rosemary leaves
70ml dry white wine
50g unsalted butter

To prepare the fish.
Remove the heads and tails, discard. Carefully remove the fillets. Set aside the bones for stock. Remove any accessible small bones from the fillets with tweezers, trim but leave the skin on. Cover and set aside in the refrigerator for later.

To prepare the stock
Put the bones in a large pan with just over 1 litre of water. Add the bay leaves, peppercorns, rosemary, celery and onion. Bring to the boil and simmer for 25 minutes. Strain, retain the stock – you should have 400ml - 500ml.

To prepare the rice

Put a large pan of water on to boil, add one bay leaf. When boiling, add the rice and cook for 7 minutes. Test – the rice should be on the hard side of 'al dente', very nearly done. Drain immediately and wash the rice under cold running water to remove all the excess starch. The water will run clear rather than cloudy when done. Drain again.

To prepare the vegetables

Finely chop the onion, garlic and celery. Put in a large pan with 2 tablespoons of olive oil over medium heat and cook until tender but do not brown (about 3 minutes). Ultra-finely slice the leek, finely dice the peppers. Add to the pan with 1 bay leaf, cover and cook for 2 minutes. Finely zest and juice the lemon, add to the pan. Stir in the saffron. Add the cooked rice, pimiento and thyme leaves. Season generously, mix thoroughly. Keep warm.

To cook the clams and to prepare the sauce

Wash the clams under cold running water and drain - remove any open ones and discard. Finely chop the shallots and the garlic, put in a pan with a little olive oil on high heat. Add the bay leaf, garlic, rosemary leaves and clams. Add 200ml prepared fish stock and cover immediately. Steam the clams on high heat until the majority have opened. Take the clams out of the pan with a strainer and set aside in a dish. Leave the pan on the heat, add the rest of the stock (200ml is about right) and the wine. Reduce to one quarter.
Discard any unopened clams and remove the clams from their shells, set aside. When the stock has reduced sufficiently, whisk in the butter and season. Strain, retaining the sauce. Put into a small pan on low and add the clams to the sauce.

To serve

Lightly oil the fillets, pan fry, skin side down in hot oil for 2 minutes, finish under a hot grill (2 - 4 minutes depending on thickness) until just done. Drizzle with olive oil, lemon and specks of dried pimiento pepper. Serve with the rice and clam sauce.

Grilled swordfish, spiced peaches, white beans, ginger and lime

This is quite a delicate dish, the background flavours of the swordfish and beans are contrasted by subtle spices, the piquancy of lime and the sweetness of peach.

400g swordfish fillet (no bones no skin)

500g cooked white butter beans
Fresh ginger root (4cm length)
2 limes
1 sweet orange
4 ripe peaches
1 scallion
Handful fresh basil leaves
100g caster sugar
2 star anise spice
½ nutmeg (grated)
Extra virgin olive oil
Freshly grated black pepper
Sea salt flakes

Finely grate the ginger, divide in half. Zest and juice the orange. Peel the peaches. Put the skins in a small pan with the sugar, half the ginger, star anise, nutmeg, orange zest and juice and 250ml water. Put on low heat and simmer for 7 minutes. Strain through a conical sieve, press all the juices from the skins. Put the liquid into a bowl. Finely slice the peaches, add to the bowl. Leave to marinate.

Finely zest and juice the limes. Finely slice the basil and the scallion (cut and reserve some short lengths for the garnish). Put the cooked beans in a bowl, season with black pepper. Add the lime zest, basil, 2 tablespoons of the lime juice, the remaining half of grated ginger and the scallions. Cut the swordfish into portions and sauté in olive oil on medium heat for 2 minutes each side (depending on thickness). Season with salt flakes and freshly ground pepper. Leave to stand for 1 minute.

Serve with the spiced peaches, white beans, olive oil and lime juice, garnish with basil and scallion strips.

Red mullet, wilted radicchio, rosemary and orange

The vibrant colour of this dish represents to us the heat of the Andalucian summer and this is when we tend to serve it. It needs nothing else except a glass of good robust white wine, such as a Godello from Galicia.

4 red mullet (cleaned and scaled)
2 heads red radicchio
1 small cooked beetroot (fresh)
1 large sweet orange
1 tablespoon white wine vinegar
1 tablespoon caster sugar
50g unsalted butter
1 onion (diced)
1 bay leaf
1 tablespoon fresh rosemary leaves
1 onion (finely chopped)
Extra virgin olive oil

To prepare the fish and orange dressing
Remove the heads and tails, discard, Carefully remove the fillets. Set aside the bones. Remove any accessible small bones from the fillets with tweezers, trim but leave the skin on. Break the fish bones in two and put in a small pan with a little olive oil, the onion, bay leaf and half the rosemary leaves. Heat to colour the onions. Add 200ml water and simmer for 10 minutes until well reduced. Finely zest and juice the orange. Add to the pan with the vinegar and sugar. Simmer for another 10 minutes. Strain through a conical sieve and then through a fine sieve. Return to the pan, whisk in the butter. Season with black pepper.

Finely chop the remaining rosemary leaves. Trim the radicchio and separate out the leaves. Sauté in olive oil in a large shallow pan on medium heat until wilted. Season and set aside. Remove the peel from the cooked beetroot and dice finely. Sauté in a little olive oil for 1 minute. Set aside.

To serve, lightly oil the fillets, pan fry, skin side down in hot oil for 2 minutes, finish under a hot grill until just done. Serve with the radicchio, beetroot and orange emulsion, drizzle with olive oil, scatter with the chopped rosemary.

Roasted guinea fowl, chickpeas, prunes, tomatoes and thyme

This is a simple yet delicious country dish - a one pot meal, quick and easy to prepare. Chickens used instead of guinea fowl work just as well.

2 whole guinea fowl(cleaned)
2 onions
3 fresh bay leaves
2 lemons.
2 tablespoons dried oregano

Extra virgin olive oil (plenty)
Freshly ground black pepper
Salt

8 shallots
3 cloves garlic
2 sticks celery
4 vine tomatoes
16 prunes (no stones)
Small bunch parsely
400g chickpeas cooked and drained
1 tablespoon brandy
2 tablespoons fresh thyme leaves
1 teaspoon ground cinnamon

Cut the birds in half with a very sharp knife and season well. Pre heat the oven to 220°C. For cooking you need an oven to table dish, large enough to take the birds with some space around and about 5cm deep. Cut the lemons and onions up into small rough chunks, spread over the bottom of the dish, add the bay leaves. Sit the guinea fowl halves on top, breast up. Drizzle generously with olive oil (100ml) and sprinkle with the dried oregano. Cover with foil and place in a hot oven for 40 minutes.

Peel the shallots. Put in a medium pan and sauté in olive oil on low heat for 7 minutes until golden. Finely chop the garlic, celery and parsley, add to the pan and cook for 1 minute. Transfer all to a large bowl. Stir in the chickpeas. Slice the prunes and add to the bowl. Dice the tomatoes and add. Mix in the cinnamon, thyme leaves and brandy.

Take the birds out of the oven after 40 minutes, uncover and distribute the contents of the bowl in and around them. Put back into the oven, uncovered for a further 20 minutes until golden. Remove from the oven and serve hot with olive oil bread.

Calves liver, brioche, red onions and Malaga wine sauce

We cook this as a first course in winter and as a main in summer - the brioche is perfect for mopping up the juices and sauce, although mashed potato is also good. Goes well with a full bodied Tempranillo from Rioja.

500g calves liver
50ml Malaga wine
2 red onions
150ml light chicken stock
50g unsalted butter
1 tablespoon red currant jelly
1 teaspoon fresh thyme leaves
100ml extra virgin olive oil
8 -12 fresh sage leaves
12 redcurrants
Salt and freshly ground black pepper

For the brioche
400g plain flour
2 teaspoons easy action dried yeast
Pinch salt
1 tablespoon caster sugar
200ml milk
50g unsalted butter
2 eggs
Egg yolk to glaze

To prepare the brioche
Pre heat the oven to 200°C. Cut up the butter into small pieces and put in a pan with the milk. Heat until melted, leave to cool. Put the flour, yeast, salt and sugar into a large bowl. Make a well in the centre, add the eggs, milk and butter. Draw in to make a soft dough. (add a little more milk if necessary). Knead well for at least 3 minutes. Cut into small pieces, shape into rolls, brush the tops with egg yolk. Put on an oiled baking tray and leave in a warm place to rise. They should double in size (they can take 40 minutes). Bake in the oven until golden – approximately 5 -10 minutes depending on size.

Prepare the liver
Trim the edges, removing any skin, cut out any pockets or stringy parts. Slice thick or thin according to preference. Season well.

To prepare the vegetable garnish

Heat 1 tablespoon oil in a large shallow pan. Drop in the sage leaves for a few seconds, turn over, remove quickly and leave to drain on kitchen paper (they should be crisp but not brown). Season sparingly with salt. Peel the red onions and cut into eighths. Add a little more oil to the pan and sauté on low heat for about 10 minutes until tender. Season with black pepper, stir in the red currant jelly. Turn out and set aside.

To cook the liver and sauce

Rinse out the pan, put back on the heat. Heat 1 tablespoon olive oil with the butter, add the calves liver slices. Sauté on high heat for 1 – 2 minutes each side depending on thickness. Put the liver into a dish and cover. Add the chicken stock, thyme and Malaga wine to the pan, let it cook on high heat for about 1 minute or so until it has reduced by half, place the liver and juices back into the pan, coat with the sauce, tip the onions back in, stir and remove from the heat.

To serve

Place a piece of calves liver on top of each brioche, spoon the onions on top, drizzle with sauce and olive oil. Garnish with red currants and crisp sage leaves.

Oven baked lamb tagine, dates, cinnamon

This is our variation on the north African / Middle Eastern tagine. The tagine refers to the pot in which it is cooked, However the dish here is the sauce so to serve you need shallow bowls and sauce spoons. We serve the meat rare, basting it with the tagine juices rather than traditionally stewed in them. It takes quite a time to prepare but the sauce can be done ahead of time and improves as its flavours infuse.

1 leg of lamb
1 tablespoon ground cinnamon
1 tablespoon ground coriander
1 tablespoon ground cumin
1 teaspoon dried oregano
2 onions
Extra virgin olive oil
Salt and freshly ground black pepper

For the tagine
200g fresh dates
1 small aubergine
1 medium onion
4 plums
1 apple
1 cinnamon stick
100g sultanas
2 vine tomatoes
Fresh ginger root (6cm length)
2 large sweet oranges
1 tablespoon balsamic vinegar
1 tablespoon orange blossom honey
1 large bunch fresh coriander
300ml chicken stock p.246

To prepare the meat
Cut the meat off the leg in large pieces either side of the bone. Discard the fat (the smaller pieces of meat can be taken off and used separately, for example, to make meat balls). Mix the oregano, cinnamon, coriander and cumin spices together. Rub and coat the lamb pieces all over. Season well and leave to dry marinate for at least 2 hours.

To prepare the tagine ingredients

Pre soak the sultanas in hot boiled water for 10 minutes. Remove the skins from the dates, slice in half, remove the stone and thinly slice. Finely zest and juice the oranges. Break the cinnamon stick into three pieces. Peel and finely grate the ginger root. Finely chop the coriander. Finely slice the plums. Finely dice the tomatoes. Peel and finely dice the apple. Remove the skin from the aubergine and finely dice the flesh. If the skin is tough - discard, if tender thinly slice. Finely slice the onion. Put a little olive oil into a large pan on medium heat, add the onion and sauté until soft – do not brown. Tip out, set aside for later. Add a little more oil to the pan, add the apple and aubergine, sauté for 2 minutes. Add all the rest of the ingredients except the stock, coriander and cooked onion, cover and gently cook for 5 minutes. Uncover, add the stock, simmer for 15 minutes and reduce. At this point taste - you can keep reducing for a darker and thicker tagine or leave light. Stir in the onion and coriander. The tagine sauce is now ready. Set aside and cover

To cook the meat

Pre heat the oven to its highest setting 220°C. Line an oven tray with foil. Roughly chop the two remaining onions, place on the foil and put the lamb pieces on top. Drizzle generously with olive oil and wrap up to form a foil parcel. Place in the oven (middle shelf) for 15 minutes. Take out and leave to rest in a warm place for 5 minutes.

To serve

Warm the tagine carefully and spoon into the serving dishes, carve the lamb and pile the slices in the middle. Pour the meat juices over. Serve with steamed couscous or almond bread.

Seared buey fillet, juniper, radish, turnip and potato croquette

Full of earthy roots… a traditional Andalucian potato recipe, its infamous bull and kitchen garden root vegetables. Substitute beef if you like and serve with a full bodied red such as the Monastrel from Jumilla.

400g buey (beef) fillet

For the sauce
400g oxtail pieces
2 onions
2 fresh bay leaves
2 stalks celery
2 cloves garlic
6 juniper berries
8 fresh pink peppercorns
300ml full bodied red wine
50ml balsamic vinegar
1 - 2 teaspoons 100% soy sauce
70g dark chutney (such as plum p.242)
400ml chicken stock (see p.246)

For the vegetable garnish
2 red onions
8 shallots (small)
1 beetroot (medium)
4 radish
3 turnips
8 cloves garlic

2 oranges (juiced)
1 tablespoon balsamic vinegar
Extra virgin olive oil (plenty)

For the potato croquettes
1.5 kilo waxy potatoes
1 tablespoon grain mustard
100g mild hard cheese (grated)
50g unsalted butter cut into pieces
2 eggs beaten
70g fresh white breadcrumbs
70g polenta (coarse yellow corn meal)
1 teaspoon finely grated nutmeg
½ teaspoon sea salt
Freshly ground black pepper

To prepare the sauce
Roughly chop the onions, garlic and celery, put in a large pan and sauté on high heat. Add the oxtail pieces and brown. Pour in the chicken stock, add bay leaves, juniper and peppercorns. Bring to the boil and simmer for 40 minutes. Add the red wine and reduce to a quarter. Strain. Put into a small pan, add chutney, soy and vinegar.Reduce - taste, adjust seasoning and strain. You should now have a small quantity of dark red sauce.

To make the potato croquettes

Put the breadcrumbs and polenta into the food processor and grind to fine crumbs. Put a large pan of water on to boil. Peel and cut the potatoes into pieces of equal size (not too small) and drop into the boiling water. Boil until tender but not mushy. Drain and mash immediately whilst hot. Add the butter, salt, nutmeg, grated cheese and mustard. Use a large kitchen spoon to mix vigorously until smooth, set aside to cool. When cool, spoon out the potato and shape (with your hands) into large rounds about 5cm diameter by 2cm thick. Dip each round into the beaten egg, then coat thoroughly with the breadcrumb / polenta mix. Set aside on a tray, ready to fry.

To prepare the vegetables.

Peel the onions, shallots, turnips, beetroot, radish and garlic. Finely slice the red onions. With a paring knife shape the turnips and radish into small turned pieces. Leave the shallots and garlic cloves whole. Put a pan of water on to boil, blanch the turnip and radish pieces for 3 minutes, immediately plunge into cold water, drain and set aside. Finely dice the beetroot and put into a pan with the orange juice and balsmic vinegar. Cover and simmer on low heat for 7 minutes until tender. Remove the beetroot, set aside. Sauté the shallots and garlic cloves in a little olive oil on low heat for about 10 minutes until slightly coloured and tender. Remove and set aside. Put all the prepared vegetables into an oven proof dish to keep warm.

Sauté the red onions in olive oil on medium heat, until crispy. Remove, set aside to dry on kitchen paper.

To cook the buey and croquettes

Season the fillet well. Sauté in olive oil over high heat, turn and sear on all sides, turn the heat down and cook for a further 2 minutes each side. Take the pan off the heat and leave the beef to sit in a warm place for 5 minutes. Meanwhile. shallow fry the croquettes. Put a large shallow pan on to heat, pour in oil to about 1cm deep. When hot, gently lower in the croquettes. Fry until golden each side. Take out, put on an oven tray and keep warm.

To serve

Cut the beef into thick rounds, place on top of the croquettes, scatter the vegetables round and drizzle with a small amount of sauce and olive oil. Garnish with the crisp red onion.

Roasted Lamb with lentil and aubergine confit, mint dressing

This is a popular dish at any time of the year. The Spanish use lentils and aubergines in many of their traditional dishes but rarely combine them. The mint and lamb are of course, an English favourite for sunday lunch.

1 leg of lamb (not too small)
1 tablespoon dried oregano
Salt and freshly ground black pepper
2 onions
2 cloves garlic
Extra virgin olive oil (plenty)

For the confit
200g puy lentils
1 fresh bay leaf
2 medium aubergines
1 large white onion
1 large apple
1 clove garlic
1 lemon
1 dessertspoon cumin seeds
1 teaspoon fresh thyme leaves
2 celery stalks
50ml apple and rosemary chutney see p. 242

For the mint dressing
Fresh bunch mint
Pinch of salt
1 tablespoon caster sugar
1 tablespoon white wine vinegar

To prepare the confit
Finely chop the onions, celery, and garlic. Put in a large pan with 2 tablespoons olive oil, sauté on medium heat until soft. Divide in half and set aside. Peel and dice the apple. Juice the lemon. Remove the ends of the aubergine. Cut down the sides to remove a thin layer of skin. Finely slice half the skin, discard the rest. Finely dice the flesh. Put the aubergine and apple in a pan with 2 tablespoons olive oil, Sauté on medium heat until light golden in colour. Stir in the cumin seeds, lemon juice and half the retained onion mix. Season well.

To cook the lentils
Put a large pan of water on to boil, add the bay leaf. Add the lentils and cook for 25 minutes or so until soft. Drain. Put In a bowl, stir in the thyme, the chutney and the other half of the retained onion mix.

To cook the lamb
Pre heat the oven to 220°C. Line an oven tray with foil. Drizzle the lamb leg with olive oil. Season with salt, pepper and oregano. Slice the garlic and spike in pockets over the lamb skin. Roughly chop the onions, place on the foil, put the lamb on top, cover with more foil and place in the oven for 25 minutes. Uncover and cook for a further 10 minutes. Take out and leave to rest for 5 minutes.

To make the mint dressing
Chop the mint in with the salt and sugar. Keep working it together until finely chopped. Put into a bowl and add the vinegar.

To serve.
Warm the plates. Warm the lentils and aubergine confit carefully. Carve the meat and keep warm. Collect the meat juices. Press the lentils into a ring mould positioned centrally on each plate. Spoon the confit on top. Layer the lamb on top of this, finish with the meat juices, drizzle with olive oil and mint dressing.

Grilled cod, creamed potatoes, herb pesto

This is a very simple dish where three flavours - salt, olive oil and garlic - usually found in the backgound come to the fore. Whether using fresh or salt cod, creamed potatoes accompany the fish perfectly. Try this dish with a Verdejo from Rueda.

1 kilo slab thick salt cod (or fresh cod if preferred)

For the vegetables

2 vine tomatoes

4 cloves garlic

8 closed cap mushrooms

1 small courgette

1 lemon (juiced)

Extra virgin olive oil

Salt

Freshly ground black pepper

Fresh herb pesto p.242

Parsley oil p.243

For the potatoes

1.5 kilo potatoes

70g unsalted butter

Sea salt

To prepare the cod

If using salt cod, rinse off the salt, soak in water (refrigerated) for 24 hours (depends on thickness). Change the water every two hours at first, then leave overnight. Dab dry, remove any bones and skin, cut into portions.

To prepare the creamed potatoes

Put a large pan of water on to boil. Peel and cut the potatoes into equal pieces, boil until tender. Drain and, whilst hot, put through a potato ricer if you have one, if not mash immediately. Add the butter and salt, mashing until very smooth. Set aside.

To prepare the vegetables

Finely dice the tomatoes, put in a dish, season with pepper, drizzle with olive oil and lemon juice. Finely dice the courgettes and sauté in in olive oil on low heat for 1 minute. Set aside. Slice the mushrooms (we stamp out the centre with a small circular cutter) and sauté in a little olive oil over medium heat. Set aside. Finely chop the garlic and sauté until golden and slightly crisp. Set aside.

To serve

Sauté the cod portions in olive oil for 2 minutes, finish under a hot grill until just done. Serve the fish with the mash, garnish with the vegetables. Put a spoonful of pesto on top of the fish. Drizzle with parsley oil, lemon juice and black pepper. Serve immediately.

Grilled sea bream with leek and herb mash, saffron emulsion

2 Sea bream each 1.5 kilo (clean and scaled)

For the mash
600g waxy peeled potatoes
200g green leek tops
1 bunch parsley (50g chopped)
70ml extra virgin olive oil

For the garnish
½ yellow pepper
12 mange tout.
New seasons fresh peas
3 small leeks - green ends

For the emulsion
3 shallots
1 bunch dill
1 lemon
70ml dry white wine
50g unsalted butter
1g saffron

Extra virgin olive oil
Salt
Freshly ground black pepper

To prepare the fish and emulsion
Cut off the heads and tails, discard, remove the fillets and trim leaving the skin on. Break up the bones. Finely chop the shallots and the dill. Finely zest and juice the lemon. In a large shallow pan, sauté the shallots in a little olive oil for two minutes, add the bones and 300ml of water, add the saffron, white wine, lemon zest and juice and reduce to a quarter. Strain through a conical sieve. Put in a small pan on low heat, whisk in the butter, cook until thick and creamy. Season.

To prepare the mash
Put a large pan of water on to boil. Cut the leeks into small lengths and boil until tender for 2 - 3 minutes, drain and dry. Chop the leeks in with the parsley and a little olive oil. Chop until very fine, set aside. Cut the peeled potatoes into equal pieces and boil until tender. Drain and whilst hot, mash immediately. Add the olive oil, leeks and herbs, season generously. Keep warm.

For the vegetable garnish
Pod the peas, finely dice the yellow peppers, trim the leeks and cut into short lengths. Blanch in boiling water, the peppers for 30 seconds, the peas for 1 minute and the leeks for 3 minutes. Plunge each into cold water to prevent further cooking and set aside. To serve sauté in a little olive oil on low heat for 1 minute.

To serve
Sauté the fillets, skin side down, in medium hot olive oil for 2 minutes, finish under a hot grill until just done. Arrange with the mash, emulsion and vegetable garnish. Season, drizzle with olive oil and serve immediately.

Contents

sweet things

Apple cinnamon custards.

This dessert is quite time consuming but is rewarding in that it not only looks and tastes good but it can be prepared well in advance.

3 apples
1 lemon
100g soft brown sugar
100g unsalted butter

4 egg yolks
200ml double cream
100g caster sugar
1 teaspoon ground cinnamon
3g sheet or powdered gelatine

For this dish you will need small round bottom moulds.(espresso coffee cups or ramekins). Line the moulds with cling film, allowing a generous overlap all round.

Finely zest and juice the lemon. Peel the apples and finely slice. What you need are as many whole rounded slices of apple as possible. Splash with a little lemon juice. Put the butter in a large shallow pan on low heat, add the apple slices. Sprinkle the brown sugar over and the rest of the lemon juice, turn the heat up, carefully turn the slices over and simmer for 3 minutes. The apples should be just done. Turn out into a bowl, leave to cool.

To prepare the cinnamon custard, put the egg yolks, cream and sugar into a pan and place over low heat. Continuously whisk the mixture as it heats until it turns thick and creamy (this can take a few minutes), do not brown – it can catch easily, particularly on the side of the pan. When done, whisk in the gelatine, making sure it all dissolves, remove from heat add the cinnamon and pour out into a bowl.

Line the moulds with overlapping apple slices, starting with a slice on the bottom and layering up the sides. Put the moulds on a tray. Fill with the custard, refrigerate for 20 minutes. Place a layer of apple slices on the top to seal the moulds. Draw up the sides of the cling film and fold over to seal. Put the moulds back into the fridge to set for 1 hour. Press any unused cooked apple and the syrup through a conical sieve. Retain the syrup, stir in the lemon zest.

To serve, turn out carefully, serve with the lemon syrup (warm) and a little cream.

Date, orange and mascarpone cream tart

This is one of our favourites - it is rich and creamy - try it accompanied with a dry Manzanilla from Sanlucar. Substituting prunes instead of dates also works well.

For the pastry
400g plain flour
200ml olive oil
50g caster sugar
1 teaspoon salt
50ml water

250g mascarpone
200ml double cream
50g icing sugar

For the cooked filling
2 large sweet oranges
300g dates
300ml double cream
6 egg yolks
150g sugar

For this recipe you will need a tart tin (30cm diameter). You can substitute butter for olive oil if preferred. Preheat the oven to 200°C. To make the pastry, put the flour into a large bowl, mix in the salt and sugar. Add the olive oil and water, bring together with the hands until it 'holds'. Do not over work. Press into the greased tart tin, working with the fingers and base of palms to mould a fine layer of pastry to its base and sides. Don't worry if it splits, just patch up.

Put the egg yolks, cream and sugar into a pan and place over low heat. Continually beat the mixture with a whisk until it turns thick and creamy (this can take a few minutes – it is very important not to brown – it can catch easily, particularly on the side of the pan). Remove from the heat and pour out onto the bottom of the tart.

Finely zest and juice the oranges. Remove the stalk end and stones from the dates and slice finely. Put in a pan with the orange juice, cover and simmer on low heat for 5 minutes until soft. Transfer the dates and any remaining juice to the food processor, add the orange zest and pulse until roughly mashed, Spoon the date mixture onto the custard, distributing it evenly throughout, don't mix around, leave in small dollops if necessary. Put the tart onto an oven tray. Cover with a sheet of baking parchment (do not let it touch the custard). Put in hot oven lowest shelf and bake for 25 minutes. Remove and leave to cool.

Whisk the double cream fold in the mascarpone and icing sugar. Spread over the top of the tart. This tart can be served on its own or with fresh sweet orange segments that have been dipped in syrup.

Geranium panne cotta with raspberries

A variation on the Italian classic - the geranium infuses a perfume that pairs perfectly with the slight tartness of ripe raspberries.

250ml full cream milk
250ml double cream
150g caster sugar
10 rose geranium leaves
10g gelatine sheet or powder

100g fresh raspberries
4-6 small moulds

Put the milk and geranium leaves into a medium pan and place on a low heat, bring to a simmer, remove from heat and leave to infuse for about 15 minutes. Remove the leaves, add the cream and whisk in the sugar. Bring back to simmer. Remove from the heat and whisk in the gelatine. Pour into individual moulds (here we have used round - bottomed expresso cups). Leave to cool, cover and refrigerate for two hours. Turn out using a small palette knife. You can help this by placing the mould in very hot water for a few seconds. Serve with fresh raspberries.

Chestnut mousse with red fruits

During the late autumn the sweet chestnuts are harvested in the forest areas of Andalucia. As Christmas approaches they appear on street corners all over the region in a smoking barrels. They are eaten roasted with salt, out of paper cones. This is a nice light dessert to serve during the festive season.

100ml double cream
3 eggs
100g plus 50g caster sugar
250g chestnut purée

Separate the eggs. Put the yolks, 100g sugar and cream into a pan on low heat. Whisk until the mixture turns thick and creamy (make sure it doesn't burn). Whisk in the chestnut purée, set aside to cool. Put the whites into the food processor and whisk until foamy and full. Whilst on, add 50g sugar in a steady stream, continue whisking on medium for 1 minute until silky. Turn down to the lowest setting and whisk/fold in the chestnut mixture. Spoon into small cups or ramekins. Cover and chill. Serve with red fruits such as strawberries, redcurrants and blackberries.

Note. This mousse just holds without the use of gelatine but needs to be eaten within a few hours. If in any doubt you can add a few grams of gelatine into the hot custard just before the chestnuts are whisked in.

Plum bread and butter pudding

This is a very popular pudding and although time consuming, can be made well in advance.

1 kilo ripe plums
2 medium apples
1 large sweet orange
12 slices sandwich loaf white (approximate)
400ml double cream
4 large eggs
200g caster sugar (plus a little extra for syrup)
125g unsalted butter
150g soft brown sugar

For this recipe you will need an oven proof baking dish - preferably glass about 30cm x 20cm x 4cm deep. You will also need a larger dish (that can be metal) to use as a Bain Marie. It needs to be deep enough to hold water and the baking dish.

Prepare the fruit. Juice the orange. Peel and finely dice the apples. De-stone and finely slice the plums. Put the orange juice, plum slices and the diced apples in a large pan, cover and stew gently until soft. Drain, retain the fruit and liquor. Put the liquor back into the pan with a little caster sugar and heat to a light syrup.

Put the cream, caster sugar and eggs into a bowl and whisk to mix thoroughly. Melt the butter. Remove the crusts from the bread. Put the crusts and brown sugar into the food processor and grind to fine crumbs.

To construct dip the crust-less bread slices into a little melted butter and line the bottom of the baking dish. Pour over a little egg / cream mix. Prick the bottom bread layer with a fork to allow the mix to soak in. Spoon in the cooked plums and apples, spread in a layer. Dip more crust-less bread slices into the melted butter and layer over the fruit. Pour over more egg/cream mix, prick with a fork to soak in. Tip the brown sugar crumbs over the top and drizzle any remaining melted butter over them. At this point you can refrigerate the pudding until cooking - it is better to leave for at least 6 hours.

To cook, preheat the oven to 190°C, place the dish in your Bain Marie, fill the outer dish with water (about half way), loosely cover with foil without touching the pudding. Bake in the oven (centre shelf) for 35 minutes, remove the foil and cook for a further 10 minutes until golden. Serve hot with cream and plum syrup.

Mango, cardamom and coconut tart

180g plain flour
180g desiccated coconut
200ml olive oil
70g caster sugar
1 teaspoon salt
50ml water

1 extra large perfectly ripe mango
(or two smaller ones)
6 cardamom pods
50g caster sugar
50ml hot boiled water

250ml double cream
6 egg yolks
150g sugar
1 vanilla pod

individual tart tins approximately
8cm diameter

Pre heat the oven to 190°C. To make the pastry, put the flour and coconut into a large bowl, mix in the salt and sugar. Add the olive oil and water, bring together with the hands until it 'holds'. Do not over work. Press into the oiled tart tins, working with the fingers to mould a fine layer of pastry, working out from the centre of the base and up the sides of the tin. Don't worry if it splits, just patch up. Place the tarts on a baking tray and bake in the oven for about 5 - 7 minutes (centre shelf) until light golden (check as they brown easily). Remove from the oven, leave in their tins to cool.

To make the vanilla crème, put the vanilla pod in hot water for 1 minute. Split the pod lengthways with a sharp knife and scrape out all the seeds. Put the cream, vanilla pod and seeds into a pan over low heat. Warm to infuse. Whisk in the egg yolks and sugar, continually whisk as the mixture thickens (this can take a few minutes – it is very important not to brown any part – it can catch easily, particularly on the side of the pan). Remove from the heat and pour into a bowl to set.

To prepare the mango, put the cardamom pods in a small pan with the hot boiled water, leave for two minutes and then split to release the seeds into the water. Peel the mango and cut down either side of the pip to remove the two large halves. Remove the remaining pieces. Finely slice all the flesh, set aside in a dish. Squeeze the remaining flesh and juice from the pip (the hands are good for this) and add to the cardamom pan. Add the sugar, Stir over low heat, simmer for two minutes and cool. Strain, pour the syrup over the mango slices. Remove a few of the seeds and add to the mango.

To serve, fill the tarts with the vanilla crème before removing them from the tin. Place the tarts on a serving plate, arrange the mango slices on top, drizzle with syrup and serve with sorbet see p.204

Chocolate layer torte

The first half of our chocolate duo - for its partner in crime see p.224

For the torte
100g 70% dark chocolate
70g organic cocoa
2 tablespoons corn flour
6 egg whites
300g caster sugar

For the coating
3 egg yolks
100ml double cream
100g 70% dark chocolate
100g unsalted butter
100g caster sugar

For the filling
250ml double cream
250ml mascarpone

Pre heat the oven to 190°C. Break up the chocolate, put into a bowl over boiling water to melt. Put the egg white into the food processor and whisk until full and frothy. Add the sugar in a steady stream and whisk on high for about 3 minutes until silky and stiff. Turn down to medium and, whilst on, add the cocoa powder, corn flour and melted chocolate. Mix thoroughly and turn out onto an oven tray lined with silicone sheet or parchment paper. Bake in the oven, middle shelf, for about 12 minutes (check after 8 minutes – when done it should be just firm to touch). Remove from oven and leave to cool.

To make the covering, melt the chocolate and the butter. Put the cream, sugar and egg yolks in a pan over low heat. Whisk continuously until thick and creamy – do not burn. Add the butter and chocolate, continue whisking vigorously until thoroughly combined, thick and glossy, Turn out into a bowl.

Whisk the cream until stiff, add the mascarpone in small amounts until well mixed.

To construct the torte. Cut the baked chocolate into 3 equal strips. Lift up one of the strips(a long fish spatula is good) and place carefully onto a tray or large flat serving plate. Spread half the cream / mascarpone mix evenly over the top. Place another layer of chocolate on top of the cream. Layer the other half of cream and finally the third layer of chocolate. Cover the entire torte with the covering, working with a palette knife (dip in hot water to achieve a smooth surface). Immediately refrigerate to set. When set, the torte can be covered and will keep well for up to 4 days. Slice to serve.

Fig and honey ice cream

This is a very quick ice cream to make, the honey makes it set soft and there is no need to churn whilst freezing. We use our local orange blossom honey made by the bees on the opposite hill. It is delicate and fragrant but any honey will have the same effect.

250ml double cream
2 whole eggs
2 tablespoons orange blossom honey
4 - 6 large ripe figs

Pour the cream into a large pan. Add the eggs, whisk until frothy. Whisk in the honey. Place the pan over low heat, whisk constantly until the mixture thickens. Be careful not to burn. Set aside to cool a little. Meanwhile de-skin the figs and mash the fig flesh into the honey mixture, whisk again and pour into a freezer proof tub. Freeze for 24 hours.

Serve with fresh figs and a good, light dessert wine such as Jarel from Competa.

Figs in raspberry jelly

Another simple recipe using figs - the textures and flavours work well together with the light jelly just holding the figs in place

2 large oranges
100g raspberries
1 lemon (juiced)
100ml apple juice
100g caster sugar
6 fresh figs
4 gelatine sheets or 4g powdered sachets

For this recipe you will need 4 glasses each with a capacity of 150ml at approximately two thirds full.

Trim the fig tops and slice in half. Place 3 fig halves in each glass (with the insides outwardly facing) and set aside.

Finely zest and juice the oranges. Put in a pan with the apple juice, lemon, sugar and raspberries. Simmer for 2 minutes, mash the raspberries into the liquid and continue to simmer for 1 minute. Strain - measure 400ml and put back into the pan on low heat. Add the gelatine (if using sheets, break up before adding) - use a small whisk to make sure all has dissolved. Remove from the heat and pour evenly into the glasses over the figs. Put in the fridge to set.

Salad of watermelon, pear, peach and cherries

Watermelons are abundant in midsummer and everyman with a plot of land grows them. Alongside come the peaches in all shapes and sizes including a squashed looking variety called 'Paraguay' with white flesh and a beautiful floral scent.

Watermelon (a quarter piece)
3 pears
3 peaches
16 cherries
Cape gooseberries (garnish)

1 large lemon (juiced)
100ml water
2 tablespoons caster sugar

Peel the pears, rub with a little lemon juice. Put the skin into a pan with the sugar, water and lemon juice. Heat over low heat for 5 minutes. Mash the skins into the liquid. Strain through a conical sieve, press firmly to extract all the syrup. Finely slice the pear flesh and leave to sit in the syrup. Peel the peaches and finely slice the flesh. Pit the cherries and cut in half. Remove the skin from the watermelon, cut into long chunks, remove the pips and slice. Layer the fruit in the glasses, pour the remaining syrup over. Garnish with cape gooseberries

Marinated dried fruits with rosewater

A floral dessert of Arab origins, good to have on stand-by as it lasts for weeks and gets better and better.

2 large apples
1 large lemon
150g dried organic apricots
150g dried organic prunes (stoneless)
70g dried organic sultanas
70g dried organic cranberries
100g caster sugar
100ml organic rosewater
1 cinnamon stick
20g flaked almonds

Soak all the dried fruits(separately) for 20 minutes in hot boiled water. Peel and dice the apples, put in a pan. Juice the lemon and add to the pan with 2 tablespoons sugar. Put on low heat, cover and cook for 2 minutes. Turn out into a large bowl and cover immediately. Drain the dried fruits. Slice the apricots and prunes. Carefully mix in with the apple. Put the rosewater, cinnamon and remaining sugar into a pan over low heat, cook for 1 minute to form a light syrup. Pour over the fruits. Store in a container with a lid and leave to marinate. These fruits improve over time and can last for weeks refrigerated. Serve them with a little syrup and nutmeg ice cream, see p,204. Sprinkle flaked almonds on top.

Fresh cherry and almond frangipane tart

The cherry season is quite short in mid summer but the cherries are huge and delicious - we do very little to them except to let them sink into the fresh almond frangipane.

For the pastry
400g plain flour
200ml olive oil
50g caster sugar
1 teaspoon salt
50ml water
1 kilo fresh cherries
100ml kirsch
100g caster sugar

For the frangipane
400g whole almonds
200g caster sugar
100g unsalted butter
4 eggs separated

For this recipe you will need a tart tin (30cm diameter) or about 6 individual small ones. You can substitute butter for olive oil if preferred. The cherries are added just before serving.

To make the pastry. Preheat the oven to 190°C. Put the flour into a large bowl, mix in the salt and sugar. Add the olive oil and water, bring together with the hands until it 'holds'. Do not over work. Press into the oiled tart tin(s). Work with the fingers and base of palms to mould a fine layer of pastry, working out from the centre and up the sides of the tin(s). Don't worry if it splits, just patch up.

To make the frangipane, put the almonds and half the sugar into the food processor, grind to fine crumbs. In a large bowl, cream the butter and the remaining sugar, beat in the egg yolks. Add the ground almond mix. Whisk the egg white to a stiff peak and fold into the mixture. Spread onto the base of the tart(s). Put the tart(s) onto an oven tray. Place a sheet of baking parchment on top (do not let it touch the almond mixture) and put in hot oven on low shelf and bake for 20 - 25 minutes. Remove and leave to cool slightly.

Pit the cherries and put into a large bowl. Put the kirsch in a small pan with the sugar and heat to a light syrup on low heat (simmer gently for 3 minutes). Pour over the cherries. To serve, pile the cherries on top of the tart(s) and serve with crème fraiche.

Lavender meringues with strawberries

We harvest our lavender in early spring when the strawberries are at their best - although this is probably a summer dessert the two flavours are inextricably linked and bound by the sugar.

400g caster sugar
5 large free range egg whites
1 drop organic lavender essential oil

250g fresh strawberries
250ml double cream

Pre heat the oven to 110°c. Line an oven tray with baking parchment or a silicone sheet.

Put the egg whites into a food processor with whisk attached. Whisk on medium - high until full and frothy. Keep on and slowly pour the sugar onto the egg whites in a steady stream. Continue whisking for 5 – 7 minutes on medium - high. Lastly, carefully drop in the lavender essential oil with a pipette. When done the meringue should be silky and stiff. Spoon the meringue in small dollops onto the tray (not too close together). Bake for approximately two hours, middle shelf until crisp. Remove from the oven and cool.

To serve layer with whipped cream and sliced fresh strawberries.

Poached pears with rice pudding

This is a delicately flavoured pudding, the rice providing a perfectly creamy and textured backdrop to the fragrant, floral pear.

250ml short grain rice
250ml full cream milk

6 egg yolks
250ml double cream
100g caster sugar

6 small pears (ripe but firm)
1 lemon
200ml orange Muscat dessert wine
50ml water
150g caster sugar

To make the rice pudding put the rice and milk in a pan and cook until just done. Set aside. Finely zest and juice the lemon. Put the egg yolks, lemon zest, cream and sugar into a pan and cook over low heat, whisking continuously until thick and creamy. Stir in the rice. Mix thoroughly and spoon into small individual moulds (alternatively you can set in one mould and spoon out the rice to serve).

Carefully peel the pears with a potato peeler, leaving the stalk in place. Coat them in a little lemon juice. Slice a small amount off their base so that they can stand upright. To poach the pears you need a pan that is just the right size to hold them upright and tall enough to allow the liquid to cover them during cooking. Put the orange Muscat, lemon juice, water and sugar into the pan and put on medium heat until a light syrup has formed. Carefully lower in the pears and poach, simmering gently for 10 - 15 minutes. Set aside to cool.

Serve the dessert cold, placing a pear on top of the out turned pudding(s), drizzle with the Muscat syrup.

Photo Note. The burnt effect to the top of the pudding can be achieved with a blow torch or by holding the out turned puddings very close to a hot grill for a few seconds. The red colour by the base of the rice is raspberry syrup.

Apple strudel with almonds and cinnamon

We have been making these for a long time - they continue to go down well and taste even better when made in the autumn using newly harvested apples and almonds.

6 large apples
1 lemon
1 orange
100g caster sugar

Filo pastry approx 12 sheets
30g melted butter for brushing
Ground cinnamon to dust
Icing sugar to dust

200g ground almonds
80g caster sugar
50g unsalted butter (melted)
1 egg white

Pre heat the oven to 190°C. Peel and dice the apples. Finely zest the orange and lemon (about half the whole fruit zest is needed) and then juice. Put the juice, zest, apples and sugar in a pan over low heat. Cover and cook for 3 minutes. Turn out into a large bowl and cover immediately.

In a food processor, whisk the egg white until frothy and full. Whilst on, add the sugar in a steady stream, add the ground almonds and the butter. Scoop out the paste and set aside.

Drain the apples, set the liquid aside in a small pan. Set out the sheets of filo pastry. Cut a strip from one end and place in the middle of the rest of the sheet (this makes a double layer to the base of the strudel). Spoon (about three teaspoons) of almond paste in a line - in the centre. Spoon two heaped tablespoons of apple on top, dust with cinnamon. Brush the edges of the filo with melted butter and fold the two larger sides up and over in two layers. Fold the other layers underneath. Brush the top with butter. Do the same to make more strudels. Place on a parchment / silicone lined baking sheet, bake in the oven, middle shelf for 15 minutes or until golden brown. Remove, dust with a little icing sugar and cinnamon, serve warm.

To serve a citrus apple sauce with this dish. Take the drained syrup from the apples, put back on the heat. Add 20g unsalted butter and whisk whilst simmering until reduced to half.

Malaga wine ice cream with olive oil shortbread

This is a favourite in the restaurant - the shortbread is very 'short' made with olive oil and almonds giving it a unique flavour. The ice cream is soft and delectable.

For the ice cream
800ml double cream
300g white caster sugar
6 eggs
100ml Malaga wine (sweet and full raisin flavoured)

In a large pan, combine eggs, cream and sugar. Whisk thoroughly and place on low heat. Constantly whisk whilst the mixture slowly cooks to a thick custard. Be careful not to let it burn. Remove from heat and whisk in the Malaga wine, put into a container and freeze. After 24 hours you can scoop straight from the freezer.

For the short bread
2 tablespoons plain flour
2 tablespoons ground almonds
2 tablespoons caster sugar
2 tablespoons extra virgin olive oil
2 tablespoons Malaga raisins or sultanas
Pinch of salt

Pre heat the oven to 190°C. Combine all the dry ingredients and mix well. Add the oil, mix together to form stiff paste. Press firmly into small silicone moulds. Bake middle shelf for about 7 minutes until shortbread just starts to colour. Take out of oven, leave to cool before carefully releasing from the mould.

Nutmeg ice cream

Many people think that you need special equipment to successfully make ice creams and sorbets but they are not necessary at all. If you have a liquidizer, blender or a food processor you can make a great ice cream or sorbet in very little time. The trick is to work quickly, have adequate space prepared in the freezer and to have the right balance of ingredients. You need a large heavy bottomed pan and a good whisk.

800ml double cream
300g white caster sugar
6 large eggs
2 whole nutmeg (finely grated)
2 tablespoons liquid glucose or sweetened condensed milk. (These soften the scoop as they do not freeze and will therefore stop your ice cream from being as hard as a rock).

In a large pan combine eggs, cream and sugar. Whisk thoroughly and place on low heat. Constantly whisk whilst the mixture slowly cooks to a thick custard. Be careful not to let it burn. Remove from the heat, whisk in the softening liquid and nutmeg gratings. Put into a container and freeze. We rarely churn our ice creams. It helps to work quickly and to get plenty of air into the cooking custard. After 12 - 24 hours you can scoop straight from the freezer.

Mango sorbet

2 very ripe mangos
Juice from 1 lemon
1 cup white sugar
Juice from 3 oranges

Remove the mango skins and trim flesh from around the pip. Collect all the juices. Put flesh and juices into a blender, add the lemon juice and liquidize. Put the sugar and orange juice in a small pan. Place on a low heat to dissolve. It can come to simmer but do not boil. Leave to cool a little. Add this syrup to the pulp and fast blend until very smooth. Transfer to a container, cover and put into the freezer. After 3 hours, take the sorbet out of the freezer - it should be partially frozen. Blend rapidly and quickly pour back into the container and straight back into the freezer to set.for 24 hours. Sorbets can vary enormously - to keep the sorbet on the soft, rather than hard side, add a small quantity of alcohol - gin works well as does Champagne or Spanish cava.

Contents

baking

Olive oil bread

We make bread every day and this is our basic recipe that forms the basis of many other alternatives.

500g unbleached white flour
20g easy action dried yeast
15g sugar
1 teaspoon salt
1 tablespoon olive oil
Warm water

Optional
100g waxy black olives
(de stoned, cut in half)

Pre heat the oven to 200°C Put the flour, sugar and salt into a large bowl. Mix thoroughly using your hands. Add the yeast and mix again. Make a well in the centre of the flour, add the oil and about 200ml warm water. Bring the dough together, drawing the flour from around the edges of the bowl. Add more water as necessary to bring the dough to a soft 'loose' consistency. Do not make it too firm. Dust the work surface with flour and knead the dough, pulling towards you and pushing it back – use the sides and base of palms. Knead for about 3 minutes. At this point add the optional olives. Cut dough, shape into two loaves and dust with flour. Place on an oiled oven tray and leave in a warm place until doubled in size. Bake in centre of hot oven for about 20 minutes. When done, it should be light golden and will make a hollow sound when tapped. Leave to cool on wire rack.

Pumpkin bread

A simple, healthy, wholemeal bread with a great taste. Goes well with any number of deli dishes but can also be made for breakfast with or without the pumpkin flesh.

500g wholemeal flour
20g easy action dried yeast
1 dessertspoon caster sugar
1 teaspoon salt
1 tablespoon olive oil
1 piece pumpkin flesh (6cm cube)
1 tablespoon pumpkin seeds
1 egg to glaze
Warm water

Pre heat the oven to 200°C. Put the flour, sugar and salt into a large bowl. Mix thoroughly using your hands. Add the yeast and mix again. Grate the pumpkin. Make a well in the centre of the flour, add the oil, the pumpkin flesh and about 100ml warm water. Bring the dough together, drawing the flour from around the edges of the bowl. Add more water as necessary to bring the dough to a soft 'loose' consistency. Do not make it too firm. Dust the work surface with flour and knead the dough, pulling towards you and pushing it back – use the sides and base of palms. Knead for about 3 minutes. Cut dough and shape into two loaves. Glaze with the egg and sprinkle with the pumpkin seeds. Place on an oiled oven tray and leave in a warm place until doubled in size. Bake in centre of hot oven for about 20 minutes. When done, it should be golden and will make a hollow sound when tapped. Leave to cool on wire rack.

Almond paste milk loaf

This is a lovely, soft, slightly moist bread with a hint of almond flavour. If you are a breakfast skipper then this goes very well with that first cup of morning coffee!

400g plain flour
15g easy action yeast
1 tablespoon olive oil
1 tablespoon sugar
Pinch salt
300ml warm milk
Egg to glaze

For the almond paste
150g caster sugar
50ml water
150g ground almonds

To make the almond paste, put the sugar and water into a small pan, bring to the boil and simmer for 30 seconds. Remove from the heat and stir in the ground almonds. Leave to cool.

Pre heat the oven to 190°C. Put the flour, sugar and salt into a large bowl. Mix thoroughly using your hands. Add the yeast and mix again. Make a well in the centre of the flour, add the oil and about 200ml warm milk. Bring the dough together, drawing the flour from around the edges of the bowl. Add more milk as necessary to bring the dough to a soft, 'loose' consistency. Do not make it too firm. Dust the work surface with flour and knead the dough for about 1 minute, pulling towards you and pushing it back – use the sides and base of palms. Cut the dough into four pieces - do the same for the almond paste and work it into each piece.(Don´t worry if the paste seems dry, just work it in). Do not over knead at this point. Bring the four pieces of dough back together, knead briefly and cut onto two loaves or into rolls. Place on an oiled oven tray and leave in a warm place until doubled in size. Bake in centre of hot oven, for about 20 minutes for a loaf, and 10 minutes for rolls. When done, they should be golden and will make a hollow sound when tapped. Leave to cool on wire rack.

Spiral buns with sugared fruits

We sometimes bake these for breakfast, they are best served warm straight from the oven but they also freeze well.

400g plain flour
15g easy action yeast
1 tablespoon olive oil
1 tablespoon sugar
Pinch salt
300ml warm water
Egg (1 mixed) to glaze

For the sugared fruit
1 sweet orange
1 lemon
20g organic glacé cherries
50g caster sugar

Pre heat the oven to 190°C. To make the sugared fruit, remove a thin layer of peel from the orange and lemon then finely dice. Juice the fruit and put in small pan on low heat with the peel and and sugar. Simmer for 1 minute, Dice the glacé cherries, and add to the fruit - leave to cool.

Put the flour, sugar and salt into a large bowl. Mix thoroughly using your hands. Add the yeast and mix again. Make a well in the centre of the flour, add the oil and about 200ml warm water. Bring the dough together, drawing the flour from around the edges of the bowl. Add more water as necessary to bring the dough to a soft 'loose' consistency. Do not make it too firm. Dust the work surface with flour and knead the dough, pulling towards you and pushing it back – use the sides and base of palms. Knead for about 1 minute. Cut into small pieces and roll into thin strips about 15cm long. Take each strip, brush with egg glaze, sprinkle some sugared fruits over and spiral up. Place on a lined oven tray (greaseproof paper is best as they can get very sticky) and leave in a warm place until doubled in size. Bake in centre of hot oven for about 10 minutes. Serve warm or cool.

Spiced fruit tea bread

A heathy, protein - packed tea bread that can be eaten straight out of the oven, on its own, with butter and jam or even toasted for breakfast.

250g wholemeal flour
150g ground almonds
150g raw oats
150g sultanas
12 stoneless prunes
50g soft brown sugar
20g easy action dried yeast

2 tablespoons walnuts
1 dessertspoon ground cinnamon
2 tablespoons olive oil
3 eggs
Pinch salt
Warm milk

Pre heat the oven to 190°C. Roughly chop the walnuts and the prunes. Put all the dry ingredients into a large bowl. Mix thoroughly. Make a well in the centre, add the oil, eggs and about 100ml warm milk. Bring the dough together, drawing the flour from around the edges of the bowl. Add more milk as necessary to bring the dough to a soft, 'loose' consistency. Do not make it too firm. Dust the work surface with flour and knead the dough, pulling towards you and pushing it back – use the sides and base of palms. Knead for about 3 minutes. Place the dough in one or two oiled loaf tins and leave in a warm place until doubled in size. Bake in centre of medium oven for about 30 minutes. Leave to cool on wire rack. Serve warm sprinkled with icing sugar.

Flat oregano, garlic, cheese bread

We rustle this up regularly for room service and when lucky for staff lunch - it´s good at any time of day and you can never make too much.

400g plain flour
½ teaspoon salt
2 teaspoons dried easy action yeast
½ teaspoon sugar
3 tablespoons olive oil
150ml (or more) warm water
1 tablespoon dried oregano
1 tablespoon fresh chopped parsley
½ onion
3 cloves garlic
150g mild hard cheese
Freshly ground black pepper

Pre heat the oven to 220°C. Finely chop the onion and the garlic, sauté in a little olive oil for about 30 seconds. Finely grate the cheese.

To make the dough
Put the flour, sugar and salt into a large bowl. Mix thoroughly using your hands. Add the yeast and mix again. Make a well in the centre of the flour, add the oil and about 100ml water. Bring the dough together, drawing the flour from around the edges of the bowl. Add more water as necessary to bring the dough to a soft 'loose' consistency. Do not make it too firm. Dust the work surface with flour and knead the dough briefly, Flatten with hands to approximately ½ cm thick (or less if you can). Place on an oiled oven tray. Sprinkle with oregano, onion, garlic, parsley and cheese. Season with pepper.

Leave for 5 minutes in a warm place, cook in oven lower shelf for 5 – 7 minutes, Serve immediately.

Fresh cheese polenta cake

This delicious cake has a grainy texture and background bite from the polenta, the cheese keeps it moist and the lemon adds tang. Perfect for tea, coffee or picnic.

5 eggs
250g fresh cheese (cow's milk)
280g caster sugar
75g extra virgin olive oil
200g wholemeal maize flour
120g plain white flour
125g coarse ground maize (polenta)
30g white sesame seeds
3 lemons
Pinch salt

Whisk the eggs a little and grate the cheese. Finely zest and juice the lemons. Put the dry ingredients into a large bowl. Make a well in the centre and add all the other ingredients. Fold in thoroughly. Turn out into an oiled flan tin (approx 30cm diameter). Refrigerate for 30 minutes. Pre heat the oven to 190°C and bake for about 30 minutes. Leave to cool, turn out and serve with crème fraiche.

Mulberry custard tarts

Fruity and luscious

For the pastry
280g flour
110g caster sugar
Pinch salt
100g melted butter
3 tablespoons cool water

250g mulberries
2 tablespoons caster sugar

for the rich custard
4 egg yolks
55g white caster sugar
100ml double cream

To make the pastry
In a large bowl mix flour, sugar and salt. Pour in the melted butter and mix with finger tips to form fine crumbs. Add water and draw together to form dough. Take small balls and press into small greased tart moulds. Refrigerate for 30 minutes. Pre heat the oven to 190°C, bake for about 10 minutes until just turning golden. Take out and cool.

To make the custard, put the eggs, sugar and cream into a non - stick, medium sized saucepan and whisk continuously over low heat until thick and very smooth. Pour into a bowl to cool.

Prepare the mulberries, leaving whole or cut in half depending on the size of tart. Take some (4 - 6) and mush with the sugar – put in a small pan on very low heat and cook until the sugar has dissolved and a light syrup has formed. Strain and coat the remaining mulberries with the syrup.

To serve, fill the tarts generously with custard and prepared mulberries. Serve immediately.

Chocolate hazelnut tart

This is without doubt rich, luxurious and intense There are only two chocolatey recipes in this book and neither are done by half. Both are out to impress - this one for the girl to cook to get the guy and the other on p.185 for the guy to cook to get the girl...or so I am told!

250ml double cream
150g caster sugar
6 egg yolks
200ml sweetened condensed milk
100g 70% dark chocolate
2 tablespoons 100% organic cocoa powder
100g whole hazelnuts

For the pastry
400g plain flour
150g caster sugar
200ml olive oil
2 tablespoons warm water

Pre heat the oven to 190°C. To make the pastry put the flour and sugar into a large bowl. Add the olive oil and water and combine quickly to form a dough. Do not over work. Flatten the dough with your hands and press into an oiled flan tin (approx 24 cm diameter). Keep pressing, spreading it out and up the sides of the tin. Don´t worry if it splits, just patch up. Refrigerate whilst preparing the filling.

Warm the cream in a saucepan, break up the chocolate and add to the pan. When melted, stir in the sugar and sweetened condensed milk. Remove from heat and whisk in the eggs. Add 80g hazelnuts and pour into the tart. Roughly chop the remaining nuts and sprinkle on top. Bake in the oven middle to low shelf for about 35 minutes. The chocolate should be soft to touch but not liquid.

Leave to cool. Serve on its own or with whipped cream.

Orange and saffron cake

Two glorious flavours making one sumptuous cake!

400g plain white flour
300g caster sugar
1 teaspoon baking powder
Pinch of salt
150g unsalted butter
4 egg yolks
4 oranges
1g saffron
Milk to mix
150g or so icing sugar

Pre heat the oven to 190°C. Finely zest and juice the oranges. Put the juice into a small pan and add the saffron. Warm gently over low heat, add the zest. Put 30ml of this aside to make the icing later. Cut the butter into small pieces and add to the pan. When melted stir in the sugar and leave to cool slightly. Put the flour, baking powder and salt into a large bowl and combine. Make a well in the centre and add the juice mixture from the pan, add the eggs and gently fold in. Add a little milk if necessary to form a soft paste, Turn out into a 24cm diameter flan tin and bake in the oven for 30 – 35 minutes. Leave to cool slightly before turning out, then cool on wire rack

Mix the icing sugar into the retained saffron and orange juice, using more sugar as necessary to make a soft paste. Spread over the cake and serve.

Coffee turron muffin

Turron is an almond sweetmeat made in late summer with freshly harvested almonds and is tradionally eaten at Christmas time. We make it to our own recipe using whole organic almonds from our trees but there are many variations to be found all over Andalucia.

400g plain flour
1 teaspoon baking powder
200g soft brown sugar
120g unsalted butter
3 free range eggs
Pinch salt
120g turron
120ml strong espresso coffee
50ml milk
100g icing sugar

For homemade turron
(do in advance).
200g ground almonds
100g caster sugar
3 tablespoons olive oil

For the turron.
Put the almonds into the food processor with the sugar, grind as fine as possible. Transfer to the blender and blend until it starts to stick together. You will need to scrape down the sides to get it evenly blended. It needs to be so fine that the oil within the almonds starts to heat and holds the powder together. Pour in the oil and blend. Put in a container generously lined with cling film or greaseproof paper, press down frimly to make a solid piece. Wrap up and completely seal.

Pre heat the oven to 180°C. Make the coffee and melt the butter, leave to cool a little. Set aside 20ml of each to make the icing later. Put the sugar and eggs in a large bowl and whisk together, Add the melted butter and coffee. Break up the turron into small pieces and add to the mixture. Sieve the flour, baking powder and salt. Fold this into the mixture. (Do not over mix – lumps and floury parts are perfect muffin texture). Line the muffin tins with deep paper cases and spoon in the mixture filling them almost to the top. Bake in the oven, middle shelf for about 25 minutes. (When ready a sharp knife inserted in the middle should come out clean). Remove the muffins from the tin and leave to cool.

To make the icing, beat the icing sugar, remaining butter and coffee until very smooth. Drop-drizzle over the muffins.

Rosemary and anise apple cake

The anise and rosemary are both sweet and woody and their fragrance is of our surrounding hills. Although the ingredients in this recipe have strong flavours they mellow during baking resulting in an unusual, aromatic cake.

300g plain flour
250g desiccated coconut
330g sugar
1 teaspoon baking powder
2 large stalks fresh rosemary (plus small amount of sugar)
4 eggs
3 apples
60ml anise dulce (alcoholic beverage)
Milk

Pre heat the oven to 180°C. Destalk the rosemary and finely chop with a little sugar. You need about 2 tablespoons of chopped leaves. Put all the dry ingredients (except the sugar) into a large bowl and mix thoroughly. Separate the eggs. Whisk the egg whites until stiff, add 150g sugar, continue to whisk until soft peak. Whisk the egg yolks a little in a medium bowl, add 30ml anise and 150g sugar. Peel and core the apples. Finely dice one apple and put in a pan with 30ml anise and the remaining 30g sugar, gently heat until the sugar dissolves and the alcohol evaporates. Set aside to cool. Grate the two remaining apples and stir into the egg mixture. Strain the diced apple, pouring the liquid into the egg mixture. Turn this out into the flour and combine well, add the rest of the anise, and a little milk if necessary to make a soft paste. Grease a 24cm diameter flan tin and fill with the mixture. Spread the diced apple on top, pressing it in a little. Bake for approx 25 minutes middle shelf.

Leave to cool slightly before removing from tin. Can be eaten warm or cool. Dust with icing sugar and serve,

Note. Many Mediterranean countries make an anise based drink both sweet and dry. Our local one is made in Rute but you could substitute others - make sure it is sweet.

Apricot and walnut streusel cake

This is one of our favourites - it is a typical deli type cake - great with tea but also great for dessert.

400g plain white flour
300g caster sugar
1 teaspoon baking powder
Pinch of salt
150g unsalted butter (soft)
4 eggs
1 orange
150g organic dried apricots
80g walnuts
Milk to mix

For the streusel
80g walnuts
100g caster sugar
40g melted unsalted butter

For dusting
Icing sugar
Ground cinnamon

Pre heat the oven to 190°C. Soak the apricots in hot water for 15 minutes to soften. Finely zest and juice the orange. Roughly chop the walnuts. In a large bowl cream the butter and sugar. Stir in the eggs, orange juice and zest. Sieve the flour and baking powder, fold into the butter mixture. Add a little milk if necessary to form a soft paste. Drain the apricots, roughly chop and fold into the mixture. Turn out into a 24cm diameter flan tin.

For the streusel, finely chop the walnuts in with the sugar and mix thoroughly. Sprinkle over the cake. Drizzle with melted butter. Bake in the oven for 30 – 35 minutes.

Leave to cool slightly before turning out, then cool on a wire rack. Dust with icing sugar and cinnamon. Serve warm or cold.

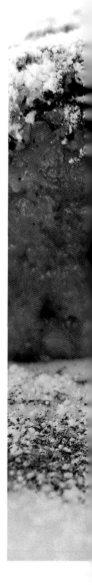

Almond macaroons

Classic biscuits - a perfect after dinner treat.

150g fresh ground almonds
150g icing sugar (or ground sugar)
4 egg whites
Small quantity whole almonds

Pre heat the oven to 150°C. Line the oven tray with non stick parchment or silicone. Whisk the egg whites until stiff, add the sugar slowly, fold in the almonds. Teaspoon the mixture in small mounds onto the tray, press an almond into each. Bake for 30 minutes in the cool oven. Remove and leave to cool. Store in an airtight container,

Oat, almond and vanilla thins

These delicate biscuits go particularly well with good, strong coffee.

100g raw oats
100g caster sugar
50g whole almonds
25g plain flour
50g unsalted butter
½ teaspoon baking powder
1 egg white
6 drops natural vanilla extract
Pinch salt

Pre heat the oven to 180°C. Line the oven tray with greaseproof parchment or silicone sheet. Finely chop the oats and the almonds. Whisk the egg white. In a large bowl cream the butter and sugar until light and fluffy. Add the vanilla, stir in the egg white, fold in the flour, oats and nuts.

Spoon in small mounds onto the tray (leave plenty of space between each mound as the mixture will spread). Bake for approximately 10 minutes middle shelf. Take out, leave to cool between batches. Store in an airtight container.

Contents 240 - 243

condiments

Harissa

Toast the whole spices (1 teaspoon cumin seeds, 1 teaspoon coriander seeds, 1 teaspoon fennel seeds) in pan on high heat for about 2 minutes, stirring constantly. Set aside to cool. Transfer to a grinder (or pestle and mortar), add 1 teaspoon dried oregano and grind to fine powder. Peel and grate 1 medium turnip (about 5cm length). Remove seeds from 12 large red chillies and roughly chop (if using dried chillies. pre soak in boiling water for 30 minutes). Retain seeds for adding heat later. Put all ingredients into a food processor, add 2 cloves garlic, 1 tablespoon lemon juice, ½ teaspoon salt, 2 tablespoons extra virgin olive oil. Blend until smooth. Add seeds to taste. Transfer to an airtight container. Refrigerates for up to two weeks.

Membrillo (quince paste)

We make this every year in the autumn from gathering the wild quinces on our site. It makes a wonderfully floral, hard set paste. Traditionally this is eaten with Manchego cheese – we serve it with fresh cheese, olive oil and rosemary straight from the herb bed. It is also excellent with cold meats and it makes a fragrant, sweet addition to roasting juices.
Wash and remove any bad parts (including blemishes) from 2kg quinces. Remove the peel and cores and put in a large pan with 1.5 litres water. Bring to the boil and simmer for 30 minutes. Add the quince flesh (roughly chopped). Add the zest from 1 lemon and bring back to a simmer - the liquor should cover the flesh. Continue to simmer for about 30 minutes until the flesh pieces are soft. Strain the liquor (this is no longer needed) and puree everything else. Measure the puree and add the same quantity of caster sugar. Put the puree and the sugar back into the pan and bring back to a simmer. Stir thoroughly and simmer for about 30 minutes, stirring constantly. (The mixture can bubble, spit and burn easily so use a long wooden spoon and don't stop stirring – even a hint of browning will spoil its delicate flavour). When very thick and deep orange-red in colour, remove from heat. Leave to cool slightly then turn out into a lightly oiled container (not metal) to set. The membrillo will set firm. Best kept refrigerated, it will last for about 3 weeks.

Parsley oil

Put 200ml extra virgin olive, 1 cup finely chopped parsley and a pinch of salt into the blender. Liquidize until smooth. Pour into a sterilized jar - lasts 5 days.

Chilli and coriander salsa

Peel and finely grate fresh ginger root (about 10cm length). Finely chop 1 bunch fresh coriander (at least 10 stalks), Remove seeds from 3 large fresh chillies (green or red) and finely chop. Retain seeds. Zest and juice 1 large orange. Put the juice into a small pan with 50g caster sugar, put on low heat to form a light syrup. Zest and juice 1 lime. Mix all the ingredients together and jar. Excellent with fish cakes. (see p.60)

Lemon and coriander mayonnaise

Put 1 free range egg, ¼ teaspoon smooth French mustard, 1 tablespoon finely chopped coriander, 2 teaspoons caster sugar, pinch salt, 1 tablespoon white wine vinegar, zest and juice of two lemons (finely grated) into the blender. Blend for a moment. Measure 500ml extra virgin olive oil into a jug. Remove the access cap on the top of the blender. Put the blender on low, pour in the oil in a steady stream. Increase the speed as the mayonnaise starts to emulsify. When fully blended bottle into sterilized jars and refrigerate.

Lemon honey mustard

Mix all the ingredients together to form a paste, 170g plain white flour, 70g ground mustard, 35g white mustard seed, 280g white wine vinegar, zest and juice from 3 lemons, 60g honey, 1 teaspoon ground cinnamon. Spoon into sterilized jars. This will keep for at least six months.

Fresh Tomato ketchup

We make this every summer when there is a glut of vine tomatoes everywhere, their fabulous taste and smell sees us through the winter. Put all the ingredients into a large pan. 2 kilos ripe vine tomatoes (chopped), ½ kilo white onions (finely chopped), ½ litre white wine vinegar, 300g caster sugar, 1 head of garlic (peeled and finely grated), fresh ginger root (2x10cm length peeled and grated), 1 large bunch fresh coriander, 2 teaspoons oregano (dried or fresh), ½ teaspoon ground cinnamon. Put on heat and bring to boil. Turn heat down and simmer, stirring constantly. Reduce until very thick. At this point the ketchup can be blended until smooth or left chunky. Bottle into sterilized jars. Keep in a cool place.

Plum and fig chutney

Again something we make every year during the summer when our plum and figs trees are brimming over. Put all the ingredients into a large pan. 1 kilo purple plums (de-stoned, roughly chopped), 1 kilo fresh figs (de, stalked, roughly chopped), 1½ kilo red onions (finely sliced), ½ litre white wine vinegar, 300g caster sugar, fresh ginger root (10cm length peeled and grated), 2 tablespoons coriander seed, 1 teaspoon ground ginger, 1 teaspoon ground coriander. Put on the heat and bring to boil. Turn heat down and simmer. After 30 minutes the fruit will be cooked and there will be more liquid. It now needs to reduce until there is very little liquid left. It will then be ready - as it nears the end, stir constantly to avoid burning. Bottle into sterilized jars.

Apple and rosemary chutney

Peel and dice 5 large apples. Finely slice 2 large onions. Put these into a large pan with 500 ml white wine vinegar, 500g white sugar, cover and simmer for 20 minutes. Uncover and simmer gently for a further hour (or so) until most of the liquid has evaporated. Stir from time to time. Meanwhile take the rosemary leaves off the stalks and grind or finely chop (should make about 1 cup). Stir this, along with 2 teaspoons ground ginger, into the boiling liquid. When ready, bottle into sterilized jars. Makes approx 4 (300g) jars.

Dressing

Zest and juice 1 large orange. Put the juice into a small pan with 50g caster sugar, put on a low heat to make a light syrup. Mix 1 dessertspoon smooth mustard with 50ml white wine vinegar and the juice from 1 lemon. Add the orange syrup, zest, fresh ginger root (5cm peeled and finely grated), 2 cloves garlic (finely grated) and 250ml extra virgin olive oil. Season with salt and freshly ground black pepper. Mix thoroughly.

Fresh herb pesto

We make our pesto by hand, it simply tastes better than using a blender. Using a very sharp knife, finely chop the herbs (1 bunch coriander, 1 bunch parsley, 1 bunch basil), with 3 tablespoons pine nuts. Add to 100ml extra virgin olive oil, 3 tablespoons finely grated mature manchego cheese, 2 garlic cloves (finely grated), salt and freshly ground pepper,

Aubergine jam

Remove the stalk end from one large aubergine. Remove the skin by cutting down in thin slices and finely slice. Finely slice one large red onion. Put into a pan with 50ml olive oil and sauté (stirring constantly) until lightly golden. Add 50ml white wine vinegar, 100g soft brown sugar, 1 tablespoon caraway seeds. Simmer gently for 15 minutes until reduced. When ready bottle into sterilized jars (makes 2 medium sized jars). Goes very well with cheese - keep refrigerated.

Gherkin, dill and white onion pickle

Put in a pan 200ml white wine vinegar, 200g caster sugar and 1 large mild white onion (cut in half and finely sliced). Put on medium heat and simmer gently for 10 minutes. Finely slice 8 medium pickled gherkins and add to the pan. Stir in 1 cup finely chopped fresh dill, zest and juice from 1 lemon and fresh ginger root (3cm length, finely grated). Bottle into sterilized jars.

Raita

Mix thick, natural, best quality Greek yogurt (250ml) with lemon juice (1 tablespoon), finely chopped cucumber (no skin / about half), cumin seeds (1 tablespoon) and chopped fresh mint (3 tablespoons). Season generously with freshly ground black pepper.

Fresh orange and ginger marmalade

Remove the outer zest from 10 large sweet oranges (use a potato peeler). Finely slice and put aside. Remove the pith (the white outer layer) from the oranges and put into a large pan with just over 1 litre water. Cut the flesh from the oranges working around the central core parts with a sharp knife. Put all the core parts into the pan with the pith and bring to the boil. Simmer for 40 minutes. Strain, retaining the liquor. Put the liquor back into the pan, add the orange zest, orange flesh, 2 kilos white sugar and 20g ground ginger. Return to the heat, bring back to a simmer, turn heat down and reduce. Stir from time to time. After an hour or so the marmalade should start to thicken,
When ready it should coat the back of a wooden spoon. To test, spoon a small amount onto a plate and refrigerate – if after 10 minutes it has formed a skin it is set ready. You will need to stir to prevent burning as it nears the end. When ready, bottle into sterilized jars. Lasts 12 months at least.

Contents 246 - 247

liquids

Light chicken stock

Remove the breasts and legs from one whole free range chicken. (These are not needed for the stock). Strip off any remaining skin including that on the wings. Cut up the carcass and put into a tall pan with plenty of room. Add 2 large onions (roughly chopped), 3 fresh bay leaves, 4 sticks celery(chopped), 3 cloves peeled garlic, 2 peeled carrots and 1 peeled apple – no core (all roughly chopped), 1 large sprig of fresh thyme, 1 teaspoon salt, 1 dessertspoon whole peppercorns. Fill to cover with water, about 1.5 - 2L. Simmer on low heat for at least 1 hour or until the liquor has reduced by half. Strain twice, first with colander and then with fine sieve. Can be refrigerated in an airtight container (3 days) and frozen (2 months).

Light fish stock

Bones (from at least two whole fish) from any white fish but particularly sea bream, bass or monkfish. Put the bones (no skin, head or tail) into a tall pan with plenty of room. Add 2 large onions (roughly chopped), 2 fresh bay leaves, 2 sticks celery (roughly chopped), 1 sprig fresh rosemary, half a bulb of fennel, 1 dessertspoon whole peppercorns, peel from 1 lemon, 1 cup of roughly chopped fresh parsley. Fill to cover with water - about 1 - 1.5l. Simmer on low heat for approximately 40 minutes or until the liquor has reduced by half. Strain twice, first with a colander and then with a fine sieve. Can be refrigerated in an airtight container (3 days) and frozen (2 months).

Vitamin boost green gunk

Bring 500ml spring water to the boil, add 200g broccoli (cut into small pieces) and boil rapidly for 2 minutes. Remove from heat, plunge into cold water. Transfer to a liquidizer. Add 250g fresh raw spinach leaves, 8 whole almonds, 20g wheat germ, 1 tablespoon sunflower seeds, 2 kiwis (de-skinned and chopped), 500ml fresh 100% natural apple juice. Liquidize until completely smooth. Refrigerate and consume within 3 days.

Energy boost drink - mango, pomegranate, strawberry

Into a liquidizer put the flesh from one ripe mango, 8 large ripe strawberries, the juice from one lime and half a litre fresh 100% natural pomegranate juice. Liquidize thoroughly until smooth, consume immediately.

Energy boost drink - pear, blackberry, cranberry

Into a liquidizer put 500ml of fresh 100% natural cranberry juice. Add the flesh from 4 ripe (peeled and cored) pears, the juice from half a lemon, 12 large fresh blackberries (or mulberries). Liquidize thoroughly until smooth, consume immediately.

Tea infusion lemon balm, geranium, oregano

For 1 litre of tea infusion, pour freshly boiled spring water onto 5 fresh lemon balm leaves, 5 fresh rose geranium leaves and 2 sprigs fresh oregano. Leave to infuse for 2 minutes.

Tea infusion, orange, ginger, hibiscus

For 1 litre of tea infusion, pour freshly boiled spring water onto 5 fresh or dried hibiscus flowers, peeled zest from 1 large orange (no wax) 4 long slices of fresh ginger root (peeled). Leave to infuse for 2 minutes.

House cocktail 1

Mix 1 measure of gin, 1 measure of Galliano liquor, 1 measure fresh lime juice, ¼ measure fresh crushed mint, ¼ measure sugar syrup, Shake over ice, strain over 2 measures Spanish cava, pour over crushed ice. Serve immediately.

House cocktail 2

Mix 1 measure vodka, ¼ measure raspberry syrup,(or grenadine), ¼ measure fresh ginger root (grated), ¼ measure fresh lemon juice, Shake over ice, strain over 1 measure Spanish cava, pour over crushed ice. Serve immediately.

index

Helen Bartlett is chef patron of

FOUNTAINHEAD
restaurant and retreat hotel
andalucia

www.fountainheadinspain.com
www.fountainheadrestaurant.com